KT-419-872

Books should be returned or renewed by the last date
above. Renew by phone **08458 247 200** or online
www.kent.gov.uk/libs

CUSTOMER
SERVICE
EXCELLENCE

UK

The Government Standard

Kent
County
Council

Libraries & Archives

C333024141

60 second solutions
MOTIVATION

JEFF DAVIDSON

David and Charles

A DAVID & CHARLES BOOK
Copyright © David & Charles Limited 2011

David & Charles is an F+W Media Inc. company
4700 East Galbraith Road
Cincinnati, OH 45236

First published in the UK in 2011

Text copyright © F+W Media Inc. 2011

The material in this book has been previously
published in *The 60 Second Self-Starter* published
by Adams Media, 2008.

F+W Media Inc. has asserted the right to be
identified as author of this work in accordance
with the Copyright, Designs and Patents Act, 1988.

A catalogue record for this book is available from
the British Library.

ISBN-13: 978-1-4463-0046-6 paperback
ISBN-10: 1-4463-0046-3 paperback

Printed in Finland by Bookwell
for David & Charles
Brunel House, Newton Abbot, Devon

Senior Acquisitions Editor: Freya Dangerfield
Desk Editor: Felicity Barr
Project Editor: Cheryl Brown
Proofreader: Nicola Hodgson
Design Manager: Sarah Clark
Production Controller: Bev Richardson

David & Charles publish high quality books on a
wide range of subjects.
For more great book ideas visit: www.rubooks.co.uk

CONTENTS

FOREWORD

'Hitch your wagon to a star.'
Ralph Waldo Emerson

This book is structured so that each of the 60 solutions can be absorbed in just a minute or less. Use it as an active resource when you find you need a little motivation on projects both large and small. If you are that rare person who is committed to taking proactive steps to stay productive, you might be inclined to read the book sequentially. To derive its full benefits, however, keep this book nearby and flip through it to quickly find solutions that work for you whenever you encounter roadblocks.

Arranged in six themed sections, the 60 solutions range from time-tested techniques to fresh and innovative insights that career professionals and people in general have found to be helpful. Jeff Davidson has written this book in an engaging and down-to-earth style, sharing insider techniques and vital lessons that he has learned over the years. You'll feel as if he is conversing with you as a friend rather than preaching to you.

Whether you are stalled on the smallest of tasks, or on major projects with long time spans, you will find *60 Second Solutions Motivation* to be both a valuable tool and an action guide for helping you to become more accomplished and satisfied with your work and your personal life. As such, I believe that you will find great value in this book.

Mac Anderson, Founder
Successories
Aurora, Illinois

INTRODUCTION

*'Real glory springs from the silent conquest
of ourselves.'*
Joseph P. Thompson

In today's ultra-competitive work environment, it is the individual who is able to display initiative who will be successful. He who can motivate himself to get started on a project and remains focused to see it through to its end will advance more rapidly in his career. The good news is, that person could be you.

motivate to be inspired to take action

DO YOU NEED THIS BOOK?

If you recognize yourself in any of the statements below, then *60 Second Solutions Motivation* is the book for you:

• You find it difficult to get started on projects that you know to be important
• You spend too much time on periphery tasks
• You're late returning important forms
• You've missed out applying for the perfect job because your CV is still waiting to be updated
• You keep putting off making a will
• You often buy your greetings cards from the 'belated' section
• You shop for Christmas presents on Christmas Eve
• You have drawers and cupboards that you have been meaning to organize
• You actually begin some projects after the deadline has passed

Behaviours such as those described above are typical signs of procrastination, the act of putting off something until a later time, either by not starting a task or by not finishing one you've started.

Individuals who procrastinate often see themselves as unproductive and lazy. They may feel anxious and ineffectual, and they have a tendency to give up too easily and too soon. They can experience guilt at their lack of action and frustration at their inability to get on. All too often, they are perfectionists, with an accentuated need for autonomy and approval, and they may have an exaggerated fear of failure. Prolonged procrastination can diminish their sense of self-worth and self-esteem, and low self-confidence will dissuade them from taking on tasks that they worry they might not be able to complete.

To maximize your potential, you need to be on the lookout for signs of procrastination and break the habits before they have a chance to form. When you persistently check your email instead of completing a project, you are procrastinating; when you let progress on lower-level tasks get in the way of higher-level projects, you are procrastinating; when you put off till tomorrow – or even next week, next month, next year – what you could do today, you are procrastinating. If you allow it to, procrastination will diminish your experience of the present. Take as an example this scenario: you bring work home over the weekend, but you never look at it; meanwhile, knowing you intended to handle it, you decline to participate in leisure activities that would have actually contributed to a better frame of mind. Procrastination can put not only your career, but also your life, on hold.

WHY DO YOU PROCRASTINATE?

The many distractions we face both at home and at work are often responsible for our failure to motivate ourselves to begin a task. If you own a computer, more information is available to you in a day than you could process in a week, a month or even a year. The simple act of communicating alone is diverting enough. At your workstation you face constant interruptions from email, Facebook messages and – the latest excuse available to you for not getting things done – instant messaging (IM). Many professionals have become addicted to IMs, which are instantaneous and persistent; an IM flashes reminders on the screen like an itch waiting to be scratched.

The modern office is not an easy place to work in, and the widespread installation of cubicles creates an environment that is rife with noisy distractions from fellow workers, which does little to help the individual whose powers of concentration are already strained. Too many office environments today actually contribute to procrastination and a decline in productivity.

whether you believe you can or believe you can't, you're probably right

When your working environment makes it so difficult for you to stay focused, it is no wonder that you may give in to your fear of failure and put off tasks that you are concerned you may not be able to complete successfully. But how do you know if you never try? Whether you believe you can or believe you can't, you're probably right, so you need to identify what obstacles could potentially interfere with your success, and plan ahead for them. Simply accomplishing one goal – achieving a small win – can give you the resolve to tackle others, making you more confident in your ability to succeed.

EACH MINUTE IS A MIRACLE

Nearly 30 years ago, a spate of 'one minute this' and 'one minute that' books began appearing, the most popular being Blanchard and Johnson's *The One Minute Manager*. Building on the one-minute theme, this book offers 60 solid solutions (one for each minute in an hour) for becoming and remaining productive. The book is divided into six parts, with ten solutions offered in each section.

the solutions are on-the-spot strategies to get you motivated

We start with the basics: adopt the right mindset, adopt more productive behaviours. These fundamentals, which have proven to be effective, build the foundation of easily initiated techniques, attitudes and actions that help keep most work and life challenges under control. From there, you'll find a variety of techniques ranging from the profound to the provocative. I think you'll be pleased to discover that none of the solutions are of the 'just do it' variety. If one solution doesn't work for you, another will.

Unquestionably and necessarily, many of the solutions offered are contradictory; for example, some advise tackling the tough issues first, while others recommend getting started on the easy things. We are all different and what works for one may not motivate another. You will also find that a strategy that proves effective today may lose potency over time, and you then have to try another approach. So, depending on the task at hand, your energy on any given day and a host of other factors too numerous to mention, one strategy will work well for you, yet sometimes just the opposite may prove more effective. The common denominator of all of the techniques is that they will help you quickly break through logjams when it comes to starting on important tasks.

Motivation is a habit that can be learned. Knowing that you want answers and results now, the solutions offered here are primarily on-the-spot strategies for getting into action. Used deftly and repeatedly, they can help you form new habits that will aid in keeping procrastination at bay. It takes insight and effort to change, but your odds of succeeding are now a lot better with *60 Second Solutions Motivation* to help you.

A number of subject matter experts need to be cited, including Dr Piers Steel, Alan Lakein, Robert Fritz, Dennis Hensley, Lynn Lively, Frieda Porat, Dr Willliam Knaus, Edwin Bliss, Daniel Goleman, Dean Smith, Robert Fulghum, William Osler, David Viscott MD, Betty Friedan, Wayne Dyer, John Grisham, Jim Cathcart, Shad Helmstetter, Dwight Stones, Susan Jeffers, Aubrey Daniels, Roger Dawson, Maxwell Maltz, Alyce Cornyn Selby, Julia Cameron, Debra Benton, Dr William Maples and Joe Sugarman, for their ideas, influence, support or contributions to specific solutions.

part
one

part one

ADOPT THE RIGHT MINDSET

SOLUTION 1
APPROACH YOUR TASK IN A NEW WAY

'We form habits and then our habits form us.'
Ralph Waldo Emerson

You are more likely to put something off if you think it is going to be difficult or unpleasant. Sometimes it helps to focus on the end result and not how you are going to get there.

Much of what you may need to do to achieve a desired outcome may not make you happy while you're doing it. Jogging for miles to lose weight or spending less to save money will not necessarily make you feel better on any given day. But eventually, when you have achieved your target weight or you have cleared your overdraft, you begin to understand that less-than-pleasing means often lead to a highly pleasing outcome.

you are more likely to put off a task if you think of it as difficult or unpleasant

When novelist Tom Wolfe passed the deadline on an article for *Esquire* magazine, his editor suggested that he write a letter, describing how he would approach the article and what he would put in it. So, Wolfe submitted a draft in letter form. By eliminating the first paragraph or two and retaining the body of what Wolfe had written, the editor had everything required for the magazine article – Wolfe had successfully defeated his writer's block by approaching the task in a new way.

You may find that it is not the task that is difficult, but the getting started on it. If you are finding it hard to begin, try approaching it from a different perspective.

writer's block the inability to begin or continue work on a piece of writing

break free of the chains that hold you back from getting started

QUICK FIX: WRITER'S BLOCK

If you're having trouble getting through that project report or analysis your boss wanted on his desk last week, try the following suggestions:

Visualize yourself completing the last sentence This will help you break free of the chains that hold you back from getting started on the assignment (see Solution 6).

Clear your work space When preparing a report or other assignment, you need to tune out distractions; working on an uncluttered surface is an effective way to do this (see Solution 14).

Outline your ideas Producing a one-page outline, or writing as few as ten key words on a page, can guide you through the preparation and completion of an article (see the highlighted box in Solution 35).

Write for a few minutes Set an alarm for four minutes, sit down, and start writing. Often you'll find that you don't want to stop, as it's the getting started that is the key obstacle to writing productively (see Solution 40).

SOLUTION 2
TACKLE PROCRASTINATION HEAD-ON

'I wasted time, and now doth time waste me.'
Shakespeare

When faced with too many things to accomplish, it is easy to procrastinate. Even mundane tasks appear more difficult when you have too much to do – and when do you not have too much to do?

even the smallest action in pursuit of a long-term goal is far better than nothing

Admit it when you are procrastinating. Don't make excuses about why you're not getting started; ask yourself, what is the real reason for your delay? Did something happen on an earlier project, or even earlier in life, that is holding you back? Are you afraid that you won't do a good enough job or that you'll fail if you try?

Keep in mind that if the task is vital, it's worth starting, even if you fail.

Frieda Porat, author of *Creative Procrastination: Organizing Your Own Life*, identifies many reasons for procrastination:
- Fear of disapproval, failure, making mistakes, being wrong
- Sticking your neck out, being noticed, not being noticed
- Confronting the unknown, committing yourself, exposing your inadequacies
- Taking on too difficult a task, getting into trouble, being less than perfect
- Being rejected, being on the wrong side, and getting criticized

Could it be that one or more of these rings true for you?

WHAT'S STOPPING YOU?

Is there an underlying reason for your procrastination? Perhaps you think a task is unworthy of you, or maybe you resent having to follow through on a promise because you weren't able to say 'no' in the first place. If you can identify the problem, you may be able to deal with it. Maybe you don't believe the job is necessary. Ask yourself:

procrastination
putting off something until a later time, either by not starting a task or not finishing one that you've started

Q1   Does the task need to be done?
Q2   Does it need to be done by me?
Q3   Does it need to be done in this way?
Q4   Does it need to be done now?

two steps forward and one step back is more often the rule than the exception

QUICK FIX: PROCRASTINATION

If the fear of failure is stopping you from getting started, try the following ideas:

Allow yourself a rough start At least you got started.
Accept it won't always be easy Recognize that lasting accomplishments usually require time, energy and commitment.
Understand that progress may be uneven Anticipate some level of breakdown and backsliding.
Don't be hard on yourself You are bound to have less successful days, but if you had made no attempt in the first place, you would have no chance of success.

SOLUTION 3
REDEFINE THE CHALLENGE

'What we love to do we find time to do.'
John Lancaster Spaulding

Generally speaking, unpleasant tasks don't get any better with the passage of time. In fact, certain jobs – such as cleaning out the stables – get *much* worse. You may find it difficult to get started on something if you think of it as being difficult, inconvenient or scary. If you reframe even the most mundane of tasks as something contributing to your long-term prosperity, growth, career advancement or domestic tranquillity, you will be far more productive.

One of the best-ever pep talks takes place in Shakespeare's *Henry V*. With his troops greatly outnumbered by the French at the Battle of Agincourt, King Henry's spirit-rousing speech inspires them on to victory. He speaks of the glory of England and how history would look back on that day, and he reframes their view of the forthcoming event as not merely a battle with the odds stacked against them, but as one of the greatest encounters of history; win or lose, they would forever be remembered as the valiant soldiers they are.

reframe to think of a task in a new context or from a different perspective

So, be your own coach, give yourself a half-time pep talk, and turn yourself around to achieve your goals.

unpleasant tasks don't get any better with the passage of time, so, if you have something to do, you might as well take care of it now

QUICK FIX: GETTING IT DONE

How, you may ask, can a mundane task be exalted? It may help you to consider that it's often not the task itself that is vital but what the task represents, such as:

• Keeping your word
• Displaying your professionalism
• Maintaining personal discipline
• Serving as a model for others
• Breaking past old barriers

SOLUTION 4
LOOK FOR THE BIGGER PICTURE

'Many are called, but few are chosen.'
Matthew 22:14

Whenever you face a task you would rather put off, try to find the greater meaning behind it. Some responsibilities you have been assigned may seem tedious and even uninspiring. Yet, your performance will surely affect your team, and what the team does will surely affect the division or department, which may affect the organization, which could conceivably affect society.

relate the meaning of your work to its impact on others

Keeping the bigger picture in mind will help you to get started on those mornings when you would rather not be at work at all.

Robert Fulghum in his bestseller *All I Really Need to Know I Learned in Kindergarten*, relates the story of a bricklayer who merrily goes about his business while other workers seem to be plodding. When this buoyant labourer is asked how he can be so cheerful toiling all day long in the hot sun, while his colleagues seem to be less than excited about their work, his response is: 'They are laying bricks; I am helping to build a cathedral to celebrate the glory of God.'

BREAKING IT DOWN

Although I have written more than three dozen books, there are days when I don't want to write a single word. I have learnt to override this tendency to procrastinate by relating the meaning of my work to its impact on others.

impetus the energy or motivation to accomplish or undertake something

Each completed chapter is one step closer to a finished manuscript; a publisher is waiting for the manuscript so he can assign the project to copy editors, then production design staff, graphic artists, and so on, to create a finished book; the book needs to be published as scheduled so that the sales and distribution team can get it to the customer. A lot of people are depending on me to do my job so that they can do theirs, and ultimately, the reader will benefit from the book we create.

None of this could happen if I sat at my office, in eloquent obscurity, drawing blanks about how to get started.

QUICK FIX: GAINING IMPETUS

When you relate the meaning of your work to how it impacts on others, you'll have more impetus to begin. On a piece of paper, sketch out a simple diagram or flow chart of how your contribution impacts on those around you, how their contribution impacts on others, and so on. Keep that perspective in mind throughout your working day.

SOLUTION 5
REFLECT ON PAST ACHIEVEMENTS

'Everything in nature is a cause from which there flows some effect.'
Benedict Spinoza

Think about the times you had trouble getting started in the past, what happened once you finally did get started, and how good you felt when you accomplished what you set out to achieve. Dig up those letters of praise you received for previous projects or look out those commendations for meritorious efforts.

being reminded of our recent triumphs can spur us on to greater success

When you can reread your kudos, or simply summon those same feelings of satisfaction, happiness and accomplishment, you may well have the winning formula for getting started on a troublesome task.

Close to where I live is the Dean E. Smith Center, the home of the University of North Carolina's men's basketball team. The banners and pennants of every accomplishment the team has ever achieved, both big and small, hang proudly from the rafters for all to see, alongside the retired jerseys of former UNC basketball greats. These symbols of past successes tell new recruits, 'We have a tradition here. We are winners, and we will win again.'

*you have the winning formula for getting
started on a troublesome task*

kudos acclaim or praise for exceptional achievement

QUICK FIX: SELF-WORTH

When you are tired and stressed, it is easy to get into a negative way of thinking and this can hold you back from achieving your best. Whenever you find yourself having negative thoughts, replace them with positive ones. Say them out loud or write them over and over if it helps.

Negative thought	Positive thought
I have never accomplished anything.	I have accomplished many things.
I always make mistakes.	I do many things well.
I am stupid.	I am clever.

SOLUTION 6
VISUALIZE YOURSELF SUCCEEDING WITH EASE

'Nothing is so fatiguing as the eternal hanging on of an uncompleted task.'
William James

Visualization is a powerful technique that can help you to focus on and achieve your goals. By creating a mental picture of yourself successfully completing a job, even the most dreaded of tasks can lay within your capabilities.

visualization
forming a mental image to foster a sense of calm and a more ready focus on tasks

US athlete Dwight Stones, the men's high jump world record holder from 1973 to 1977, avidly used visualization techniques, influencing generations of high jumpers since. Before every jump, Stones paused for several seconds to visualize his approach and take-off. He could be seen moving his head up and down, counting the steps, visualizing how he'd use his arms and upper torso to create upward thrust to a successful jump. He didn't clear the bar at every height every time – indeed, many of his jumps were misses – but failure is never the focus of visualization; success is. Using this technique, Stones broke the world record three times!

Say, for example, you are asked to give an after-dinner speech even though you hate public speaking. You put off working on your speech, knowing that on the big night nerves will make each morsel of food stick in your throat. Now try visualizing writing an effective speech, arriving at the venue, eating a delicious meal, approaching the lectern, speaking with eloquence and receiving hearty applause. This technique can help you to perform well and accelerate your progress.

role model a person who, as a result of position, expertise, actions and/or personality serves as an example of good, productive or effective conduct

FIND YOURSELF A ROLE MODEL

Here's a variation on visualization that may work for you: simple observation. Is there someone in your office (or anywhere else, for that matter) who you admire, someone widely regarded as having a take-charge attitude? This person 'takes the bull by the horns' and dives headlong into complex tasks and demanding projects. Study the behaviour of such action-takers and high achievers, and see what you can learn by observing them. When you stall on a project, ask yourself, how would the person you have identified act in the face of the task you're confronting? Sometimes simply imagining this person, and the kinds of action she would take, is enough to get you started.

SOLUTION 7
GET SCARED AND GET STARTED

'Every day, in every way, I'm getting better and better.'
Émile Coué

The next time you dread launching a new project, allow yourself to experience the full gamut of fear-related sensations from nervousness to nausea. This discomfort is completely normal – it is a typical human response to challenges that may seem beyond you.

there's no need to hide underneath the covers when a deadline looms

When regarded as routine, feeling the fear can become an important weapon in your arsenal. Hereafter, if you act anyway rather than letting feelings of fear stop you, you will be pleasantly surprised to find how much easier it is to get started.

Dr Susan Jeffers, in her book *Feel the Fear and Do It Anyway*, discusses how tasks and activities outside of our comfort zones may cause us to feel uneasy. Jeffers suggests that when you encounter a task that represents a hurdle or a roadblock, you need to let yourself feel all the emotions that arise. Are you uneasy? Is your stomach upset, are you light-headed or trembling? Do you feel fearful? Jeffers says that when you are forthright with yourself about how you feel (namely, scared), and if you take action anyway, you are often able to break through your fear and overcome the obstacle that loomed so large.

FEAR OF SUCCESS

If one of your underlying reasons for procrastination is the fear of success, then your immediate mission is to gain reliable knowledge of how this success would actually affect your career and life. Talk to or read about others who have achieved similar success, converse with associates and friends about the possibilities, or simply sketch out on paper how you see the situation unfolding – after all, your guess is as good as anyone's.

QUICK FIX: OVERCOMING FEAR

The fear of certain situations or tasks need not be debilitating. Try using the following techniques:

Recognize the fear Be honest with yourself – stop making excuses for putting off the task and accept that you are scared.

Face the worse that can happen Realizing the consequences of not taking action because of your fears – for example, facing penalties for missing a deadline, or missing out on a one-time opportunity or investment – may be all you need to kick-start you.

Get your fears down on paper By writing down your fears and uncertainties you'll begin to deflate them.

SOLUTION 8
DISCARD LIMITING LANGUAGE

'To know and not to do is not yet to know.'
Zen proverb

Some words have negative connotations: 'must', 'should' and 'ought', for example. If you were told by your parents and teachers that you *should* do something, you *must* do something or that you *ought* to do something, the chances are that as an adult, you may subconsciously regard such terms as burdensome commands, even when you use them yourself.

replace should, must and ought with choose, want and will

Each time you think 'I should, I must, I ought to do something', the energy that you have for a task is not nearly as high as it would be if you changed your internal language to positive word choices such as *choose*, *want* and *will*.

WORD POWER

Whether you think it to yourself or say it out loud to others, your use of language can affect your ability to take on tasks of all sizes. Instead of thinking, 'I must finish the ABC report by Thursday,' try replacing your language with 'I *choose* to finish the ABC report by Thursday,' or 'I *want* to finish the ABC report by Thursday,' or 'I *will* finish the ABC report by Thursday.' Notice how, instantly, your entire being realigns and re-energizes itself to aid you in your proactive choices.

UPBEAT MESSAGE

Suppose that you receive a call, and a customer or client requests a certain piece of information. Instead of saying, 'I'll have to dig up that file for you,' try saying 'I will be happy to locate that file for you.' This conveys a more upbeat message to the caller and, even more importantly, it makes the task seem far less onerous.

QUICK FIX: MOTIVATIONAL LANGUAGE

From now on, if you find yourself reluctant to handle a task and you want to see a dramatic improvement in your energy and attitude, preface your statements with:

- I choose to
- I want to
- I will be happy to

SOLUTION 9
ENGAGE IN CREATIVE PROCRASTINATION

'Misspending one's time is a kind of self-homicide.'
George Savile

Everyone procrastinates now and then, including you, whether or not you care to admit it. It is part of the human condition.

To make the best of a lingering case of procrastination, try to fill your time with efficient activity. If you are avoiding getting started on the big task you should be doing, turn your attention to all those other little jobs that you have been putting off.

Once all the little things are taken care of, there will be no excuses left for tackling the main task.

rather than frittering away the time, take care of other useful business

DO SOMETHING USEFUL

On occasion it is understandable and even desirable to do something else other than the task you had originally set out to accomplish, such as when short-term, high-priority jobs or opportunities arise. Don't beat yourself up over such incidences – they happen to everyone.

Too often, of course, procrastinators not only ignore the main task, but also fail to accomplish all the other little jobs that will eventually need their attention. They dawdle; they surf; they do nothing at all. Rather than simply frittering away the

*even the smallest
seeds can yield a
bountiful harvest*

time, it is better to indulge in a little 'creative procrastination'. As long as someone is not depending on you to complete the main task, you could, at least, be getting on with the small secondary tasks. But make no mistake, the big task will still be waiting for you, because it's not going anywhere by itself, no matter how much you want it to.

A CLEAN SLATE

If you get all the little jobs out of the way, when you eventually do begin to tackle the main project or assignment, you can approach it with the mindset that, 'I completed all of these other things and now the slate is clean to do a good job on this.' And once you finally initiate and finish the big, important task you've been shirking, think how good it will feel to know that all of the smaller, yet necessary, tasks have been done.

QUICK FIX: SECONDARY TASKS

Try to accomplish as many of the other small tasks as you can while putting off the big one that you know you need to be tackling. It's better to be doing something than nothing at all. Here's a list to get you started:

• File your paperwork
• Pay the utility bills
• Renew your car tax
• Buy new cartridges for your printer
• Fill up the stapler

SOLUTION 10
WATCH WHAT YOU SAY TO YOURSELF

'Be careful of what you say to yourself.'
Shad Helmstetter

It may surprise you to learn that much of what people say to themselves is negative. Tune in and be more conscious of the internal messages you give yourself. Replace the negative statements that you more routinely offer yourself with some positive messages.

By letting self-boosting statements into your internal dialogue, you enhance the learning process, experience less stress and feel far better about yourself.

If you have a hard time thinking of positive things to say to yourself, take time to generate a list of statements you can use, and either write them down or record them.

A MATTER OF CHOICE

When you're having trouble getting started, motivate yourself with some positive self-talk and choose to take action by listening to internal messages such as these:

In *What to Say When You Talk to Yourself*, author Shad Helmstetter says that 80 per cent or more of our internal dialogue focuses on our shortcomings. That means that most of us, all day long, are internally saying things such as, 'I didn't do that right,' or 'My collar is off,' or 'I should have never sent that email,' or 'I'm fat,' or 'I didn't do this job well,' or 'They're going to think I'm stupid.'

- I choose to feel good about what I'm about to do.
- I choose to easily take appropriate action.
- I choose to easily complete this transaction.
- I choose to feel at ease in finishing this project.
- I choose to masterfully complete this task.
- I choose to be effective in all aspects of my job.

QUICK FIX: POSITIVE MESSAGES

When you're trying to learn something new and it's taking you longer than you wanted or expected, you're feeling stressed and you'd rather put off the task than continue, don't give in to your doubts. Change negative statements to positive messages:

Negative statement	Positive message
I can't stand this.	I easily accept this challenge.
I'd rather be anywhere else.	I have mastered situations more difficult than this.
I can't do this.	I can do this and use it to its best advantage.
Get me out of here.	By tomorrow this will be simple.

SUMMARY: PART ONE ADOPT THE RIGHT MINDSET

01   **Approach your task in a new way** You may find that it is not the task that is difficult, but the getting started on it. If you are finding it hard to begin, try approaching it from a different perspective.

02   **Tackle procrastination head-on** Don't waste time making excuses for or rationalizing why you're not getting started; try to uncover what the real reason is for your delay.

03   **Redefine the challenge** You'll be far more productive if you look for the connections between the mundane tasks and your long-term goals.

04   **Look for the bigger picture** Relate the meaning of your work to how it impacts on others, and how it contributes to your team, division, department, organization or society in general.

05   **Reflect on past achievements** Remind yourself of your recent triumphs to spur yourself on to greater success.

06 **Visualize yourself succeeding with ease** By creating a mental picture of yourself successfully completing a job, you can increase your chances of success.

07 **Get scared and get started** Don't let fear debilitate you; face your worries and take action anyway.

08 **Discard limiting language** Positive word choices can have a dramatic effect on your job performance.

09 **Engage in creative procrastination** If you are avoiding getting started on the big task you should be doing, turn your attention to all those other little jobs that you have been putting off.

10 **Watch what you say to yourself** Positive thoughts lead to positive actions; self-boosting statements will help you to achieve your best.

NOTES

part
two

part
two

SET YOURSELF UP TO WIN

SOLUTION 11
RETHINK YOUR PRIORITIES AND SUPPORTING GOALS

'If a man does not keep pace with his companions, perhaps it is because he hears a different drummer.'
Henry David Thoreau

Priorities are the handful of things in your life or career that are important to you. Keep your priorities to just a few – having many priorities is paradoxical as only a few concerns *can be* of priority.

A goal is a statement that is specific to what you intend to accomplish, and by when. To be effective and fulfilled, the goals you set yourself should support your carefully chosen priorities. Change your goals as your priorities change.

successful people are confident, action-oriented individuals with clear priorities and supporting goals

ESTABLISH YOUR PRIORITIES

Priorities are the broad elements of life that often become misplaced somewhere within the high-wire, somersault-through-flaming-hoops, balancing act of daily life. The choices confronting most individuals are often similar: career advancement versus a happy home life; income goals versus income needs; and social-, peer- or employment-induced

priorities
those things most important to you

priorities versus individual wants or needs. Make sure you know what your priorities are today, and remember that they may change tomorrow.

SETTING GOALS

Each goal you set yourself should support a priority, and each priority should be supported by at least one goal. For example, if becoming supervisor is your priority, you might set goals to get to work early, contribute as much as possible around the office, and speak to your superiors about any additional tasks that need to be done.

Targeted, time-specific goals will help you to achieve your priorities. Here are some examples of well-constructed goal statements:

Goal statement To work out for 35 minutes, three times a week, starting today.
Underlying priority Staying fit.
Goal statement To increase my annual income to £42,000 next year.
Underlying priority Attaining financial independence.
Goal statement To recruit four qualified salespeople by the end of the next quarter.
Underlying priority Having the optimal size staff on board.

SOLUTION 12
STAKE YOUR CLAIM ON A TASK OR GOAL

'We may affirm absolutely that nothing great in the world has been accomplished without passion.'
Georg Wilhelm Friedrich Hegel

There is a common misperception that the tasks or goals you undertake have to be your own, devised by you, set by you, and pursued by you. In fact, it is much more likely in business today that these will be set *for* you. Key to your success will be the ability to adopt tasks and goals as your own.

without ownership, procrastination is predictable

Are you committed to the project you have been assigned? Think about a situation in which the goal is taken from you. Suppose you could no longer proceed down your chosen path. Suppose all activity in pursuit of a goal had to cease. Would you be outraged? Would you object? Would you fight for your right? If so, it's your goal.

Alternatively, if you could take it or leave it, if you wouldn't be that upset, if it all would be forgotten by the next day, if it won't keep you awake at night, you haven't claimed ownership of the task.

OWNING THE GOAL

project commitment
the willingness to take responsibility for the outcome, good or bad

When you claim ownership of the goal to complete a task or project, you organize yourself in ways that support that goal on a daily basis, and you don't need as many external motivators, such as deadlines. This is important as – just as for many of the long-term and continuing goals that you set for yourself – waiting until a minute before the deadline would be foolhardy. You can't accumulate vast sums of cash, lose huge amounts of weight, or finish writing all your reports at the last minute.

If it's easy for you to shift the blame, disassociate yourself, or pretend you didn't have any input – all easily perfected skills – chances are you were never committed to a project in the first place. If others come along and ask who's responsible and you tell them that you are, then the project *is* yours.

QUICK FIX: GOAL OWNERSHIP

If a task is assigned to you, there are many ways to make it your own, and in so doing make it more enjoyable and rewarding for yourself. Here are some ideas:

- Find the quick win (see Solution 38)
- Tackle the job one section at a time (see Solution 51)
- Assert your control by shaping it

SOLUTION 13
ASPIRE TO BE ORGANIZED

'Don't let life discourage you; everyone who got where he is had to begin where he was.'
Richard L. Evans

When you are in control of your surroundings, you have a better chance of staying focused, efficient and effective. No matter how difficult it may seem, you can maintain control of what crosses your desk and how it is handled.

being organized is the key to being productive

Simply organizing materials, whether hard copy or on disk, putting them into smaller file folders, stapling them, or rearranging the order of things often represents a good, pre-emptive move in the battle against procrastination.

LEARN TO BE ORGANIZED

The only difference between those who are 'good at organizing' and those who think they are 'not good at organizing' is that organized people make an effort to be so. There is no organizing gene. You can do as good a job as the next person. Things do not mysteriously get out of order or become lost; there is no force in the universe operating in opposition to you and conspiring to keep you disorganized; it is possible to eliminate the clutter that stops you from getting started.

OUT OF SIGHT, NOT OUT OF MIND

The over-accumulation of information on your desk and computer desktop can distract you from taking action on the task at hand. Create inbox folders and establish a folder in your filing cabinet where you can temporarily house material that you may need, and label them with months and weeks. This system enables you to regularly review surplus information when more is known.

QUICK FIX: PROCESSING INFORMATION

For each item that crosses your desk or computer screen, ask these fundamental questions:

- What's the issue behind the document?
- What does it represent?
- Why did I receive it?
- Is it important?
- Will it be replaced soon and if so, do I need to keep it now?
- Should I have received this?
- How else can this be handled?
- Can I delegate it?
- Can I file it under 'Review in six months'?
- Can I bin it?
- What will happen if I don't handle this?

SOLUTION 14
MANAGE YOUR DESK FOR DECISION

'*Challenges are what make life interesting; overcoming them is what makes life meaningful.*'
Joshua J. Marine

every evening, clear your desk and congratulate yourself on what you have accomplished today

To enhance your productivity and decisiveness, get your desk under control. Piles of 'to do' paperwork in your field of vision can be an impediment to getting started on a job. Clear your desk so that you only have the project you are currently working on in front of you.

When you have only a single task to hand, your odds of maintaining clarity and direction increase dramatically. Consider, for example, how much easier it is to focus when you are at a conference where you only have the project materials available to you.

GAINING A SENSE OF CONTROL

After you've cleared your desk, apply the same principle to your computer's desktop, your inbox, the top of your filing cabinet, cupboard shelves, and

Joe Sugarman in his book *Success Forces* argues that by clearing your desk every evening, you automatically have to *choose* what to work on the next day. It is a discipline that enables you to get started in the morning while others find themselves only slowly getting underway.

even other areas of your life – your dining-room table, your car's glove compartment, your wardrobe. The fewer things you have in these places, the greater sense of control you have over your environment. With fewer distractions, you will make more of your time.

KEEPING CONTROL

Once you have your desk under control, be vigilant against clutter build-up. Use the end of the day, slow periods or periods of low personal energy to revamp your files, order your desk, and so better prepare yourself for high-octane output when you're ready to get started again.

in major corporations, the desks of top executives remain clear and uncluttered

QUICK FIX: AN ORGANIZED DESK

An uncluttered desk enables you to focus on the task in hand. Keep the desktop clear and do not overfill the drawers. Keep a drawer for personal items, but leave entertainment gizmos at home; do include frequently needed supplies, but remember it is not a stationery cupboard. Here is a checklist of what to retain and what to toss:

✓ Telephone	✗ Plant pot
✓ Tissues and cough drops	✗ Non-essential stationery supplies
✓ Computer	✗ Photographs
✓ Essential stationery supplies	✗ Unfiled papers and magazines
✓ Notepad, pencil and pens	✗ Piles of papers
✓ Often-used forms	✗ Game Boy

SOLUTION 15
SET UP YOUR WORK SPACE FOR PERFORMANCE

'It is not necessary to change. Survival is not mandatory.'
W. Edwards Deming

The quality and ambience of your work space is at its best when it demonstrates the quality and ambience of your life – or how you would like your life to be. Recognize the importance of having your working environment support you. Take the time to create a place where you can work to your best ability, a space that you can look forward to being in. Procrastination has little chance here.

your environment can enhance your productivity, efficiency and creativity

ENHANCING YOUR WORK ENVIRONMENT
Surround yourself with plants, which convert nitrogen to oxygen; ensure that the ventilation is more than adequate; and keep a glass of water close at hand. Dehydration is a key factor for low productivity; often when you think you're too tired to begin something, you're actually only thirsty.

Keep familiar items that motivate you, such as pictures, photographs and certificates, near – but not on – your desk. Change ordinary light bulbs for daylight bulbs, and play ocean wave music if it won't disturb others.

THE ERGONOMIC ENVIRONMENT

ergonomics
the science that examines how devices should most smoothly accommodate the human body and human activity

While there is much you can do to improve your work environment, sometimes it is necessary to ask for help. Every employee is entitled to a safe place to work, and you could benefit from an ergonomic review of your working space. This will assess issues such as tripping hazards, lighting adequacy, and suitability of office furniture and computer equipment set-up. If changes are required, these are likely to be relatively inexpensive and can result in vast improvements in productivity and efficiency.

QUICK FIX: OPEN-PLAN OFFICE

It can be hard to keep your focus in an open-plan office. Here are a few ideas that can help you to minimize distractions:

- Room dividers – available in a wide variety of shapes and sizes
- Sound screen – an electronic device that creates a sound 'barrier' that masks or mutes the effects of sounds emanating from beyond the barrier
- White noise – a non-invasive, non-disruptive sound, such as the rushing water of a table-top fountain or the gentle, rhythmic whirring of a small fan's motor, that drowns out other noises

SOLUTION 16
GET YOUR DUCKS IN A ROW

'Any idiot can face a crisis – it's day to day living that wears you out.'
Anton Chekhov

If you know that there are likely to be bottlenecks in completing a job, you may be more inclined to put off getting started on it. To give yourself the best possible chance of success, you need to marshal your resources and take care of contingencies at the very outset of a project. These preparatory activities enable you to take on critical tasks confidently and will help you to attain your best results.

FAIL TO PREPARE, PREPARE TO FAIL

To not plan for what you might need before you take on a project is inefficient and likely to lead to delays along the way. Take the time to line up your requirements before you begin. This may include investing in materials or identifying key resources such as phone numbers of key contacts, URLs of vital websites, or a list of usernames and passwords. Preparation complements plotting a course (see Solution 35).

You intend to come into the office at the weekend to reorganize your messy filing system. During the week, as you pass the stationery cupboard or your local Ryman's store, you should take the chance to accumulate box folders, hanging folders, identification tags and labels, and rubbish bags, so that when Saturday comes you can concentrate on the job itself.

TAKING CARE OF THE LITTLE THINGS

It is reasonable to schedule time to take care of life's administrative tasks, such as handling correspondence, paying bills, tidying up, and keeping things in order. Some people find it advantageous to set aside a whole day solely for taking care of 'administrivia'. Thereafter, they have uninterrupted days of highly productive activity. However, the problems start when you put off doing the big jobs by using the small tasks as an excuse for not getting started.

QUICK FIX: TIME MANAGEMENT

Do you need help to effectively schedule your time? Consider investing in software specially designed for the job. For example, Achieve Planner, the time-management software for Windows, allows you to arrange tasks hierarchically and to colour-code your priorities. The distributors at *www.effexis.com/achieve/planner.htm* assert that it will help increase your productivity. This is just one of many programs available; once you find the one that works for you, stick with it.

SOLUTION 17
LIVE 'IN THE ZONE'

'Work joyfully and peacefully, knowing that right thoughts and right efforts inevitably bring about right results.'
James Allen

There are days when work seems effortless, your output is exemplary, and nothing can distract you from the task at hand. You are 'in the groove', 'firing on all cylinders', living 'in the zone'. Regardless of what you call it, wouldn't it be useful if you knew how to get into this state on a more consistent basis?

IDENTIFYING THE ZONE

Here's a simple exercise you can undertake to help you to identify and recreate the environment in which you work at your best. Review the lists on the opposite page. Circle each item that was present or was a factor when you were 'in the zone'. Now recall another good work day and read through each of the questions once again, circling relevant items as you go. Recalling a third or even a fourth time in which you were highly productive, run through the questions again. A strong pattern may have emerged. You'll know which factors are most often present on those occasions when you are at your most productive. When you are having trouble getting started on a task, use this information to emulate your zone scenarios to increase the probability of achieving great results.

in the zone the circumstances under which you do your best, most productive work

Recall a time when you were highly productive
- Where were you?
- What time of day was it?
- What day of the week was it?
- Was anyone else around?
- What was the temperature like?
- What was the lighting like?

Think about what you were like
- What were you wearing?
- What did you consume the night before?
- How long did you sleep the night before?
- What was your level of fitness?
- What did you eat that morning?

Think about the tools available to you
- Were you using a computer, a laptop, or palm-top computer?
- Were you using other equipment?
- Were you online?
- Were other resources available?
- Were periodicals, books or directories present?

Assess other factors that were present
- Did you have a room with a view?
- Were you in a comfortable chair?
- Were you at a desk or at a table?
- Were you in a moving vehicle, such as a plane or a train?
- Was there quiet, or soothing, background noise?
- What were the colours of the walls surrounding you?
- Could you hear others?
- Were you near the coffee machine?

SOLUTION 18
DECIMATE DISTRACTIONS

'Half our life is spent trying to find something to do with the time we have rushed through life trying to save.'
Will Rogers

When you find yourself in an environment that subjects you to all manner of distractions and interruptions, even the smallest of tasks can seem daunting. Sometimes the reason that you keep putting off getting started on a project is that you anticipate interruption. Once you have set upon a course of action, however, you tend to stay focused. It is crucial therefore that you devise some kind of strategy at the outset that will keep distractions at bay till you are underway.

even a mere handful of distractions and interruptions each hour can flatten your productivity like a pancake

Too many people do a reasonably good job of eliminating distractions at the start of a project. Thereafter, however, they let down their guard, then wonder why it's so difficult to finish anything; don't let that happen to you.

A study conducted by *Industrial Engineer* magazine found that the typical interruption sustained by managers lasted 6 to 9 minutes, but that the average time they needed to 'recover' from interruptions lasted an additional 3 to 23 minutes. Is it any wonder that most career professionals consider interruptions to be the most stressful aspect of their jobs?

FIELDING DISTRACTIONS

If a manager supervises six employees and each employee asks a question on average every 2 hours, he will field 24 questions a day, 120 interruptions per week – that's three disruptions each hour in a 40-hour week. By allocating the questions he receives into four categories, he can regain control of his time.

Type 1 The answer is already in print, for example in the company policy manual.
Response 'Refer to material available to you to find the answer.'

Type 2 The answer can be provided by another member of staff.
Response 'Refer to Joe Bloggs.'

Type 3 The answer is a straightforward yes or no answer.
Response 'Yes' or 'No'.

Type 4 The answer requires the manager's input.
Response 'Yes, send it my way.' 'I'll handle it.' 'You bet I'm concerned.'

By employing this system, a manager can drastically cut interruptions particularly as it encourages staff to become more self-reliant.

QUICK FIX: AVOIDING DISTRACTIONS
To be able to concentrate fully on a particular task it may be necessary to disconnect yourself from everyday distractions (see Solution 19). If you think you need an hour, ask not to be disturbed for at least 90 minutes, and:

- Hold your calls
- Don't accept visitors
- Ignore your email
- Find a quiet place

SOLUTION 19
DISCONNECT YOURSELF

'I was taught very early that I would have to depend entirely upon myself; that my future lay in my own hands.'
Darius Ogden Mills

Sometimes, to give your full attention to your task, you may need to move yourself totally away from others for a period of time. When you have resolved that any disturbances in completing your task will not be tolerated, you need to condition your environment for no distractions.

If it sounds like a luxury to be able to allocate a block of time just like that, consider the cost of putting off

when you've found the right spot, you'll feel good, productive and unhurried

QUICK FIX: DISCONNECT PHYSICALLY
Identify those places where you will be able to work undisturbed:

- Conference room
- Colleague's office
- Park bench
- Attic or basement
- Library
- Garden
- Hotel room
- Parked car
- Airport check-in queue
- Tree house

completing – or even starting on – that big project yet again. If you have to leave your workplace to get things done, most bosses will understand – after all, they're not paying you to procrastinate.

DISCONNECT MENTALLY

Once you've found the right location, you still may face the challenge of maintaining concentration. In the middle of working on a project, you'll suddenly remember that you need to be doing something else. This is the procrastination phenomenon at full force: when you're tackling something that is difficult for you, you'll think of other things you have to do. Attempt to stay with what you are doing and let all the rest go. What better use of your time is there than to complete what you have started?

> *when you're tackling something that is difficult for you, you'll think of other things you have to do*

QUICK FIX: DISCONNECT DIGITALLY

If you are constantly tempted to surf the web or check your email, try using a Temptation Blocker (*http://sourceforge.net/projects/ temp(blocker*) to 'lock yourself out of specific applications' for a specified amount of time.

SOLUTION 20
BEGIN NOW, WHICH IS AS GOOD A TIME AS ANY

'Those who make the worst use of their time are the first to complain of its brevity.'
Jean de la Bruyère

Many people believe that if they could only initiate the tasks that they have been putting off at the 'right time', then these jobs would be easier to begin and to complete; but once you acknowledge that most tasks have no perfect start time, you will recognize that the best time to begin could well be right now.

the best time to begin could well be right now

If you find yourself delaying taking action until you feel like it, be aware that 'feeling like it' is a state of mind that is more under your control than you might suppose. When will you ever actually feel like cleaning out the hamster cage? The longer you wait, the dirtier it gets, whether you feel like it or not.

I know of people who always delay starting something until the beginning of the hour, others who wait for a certain day of the week, and yet others who put off jobs for a rainy day. In many cases, the 'perfect' start time is simply another in a long line of tricks that the mind plays to give legitimate reasons for not getting started, and really these are just excuses.

WAITING FOR THE PERFECT TIME

When you receive a cheque or a complimentary letter in the post, you may regard that as a good day. Yet, whatever you did to earn the sum or merit the letter was put in motion before the day you received it.

if you find yourself waiting for the perfect moment to begin a task, you're wasting precious time

By the same way of thinking, it is erroneous to believe that there is a perfect time to start on tasks. The mental energy you need to exert to begin a task may have already kicked in long before the time you have set aside as perfect for beginning. Stop delaying and just accept that getting started now is as good a time as any.

QUICK FIX: PUTTING IT OFF

Many of the tasks you face could be tackled at this time or that with little repercussion. To break through your delaying tactics you should consider:

- It is of no concern if you fill out your report log at 8.42am rather than 9am when it's not due until the afternoon.
- The tax office doesn't care that you completed your online tax return on 31 January at 10.36am or 2.45pm.
- It is immaterial if you remove the clothes from the drier before or after the news.
- The weather makes no difference to indoor jobs.

SUMMARY: PART TWO
SET YOURSELF UP TO WIN

11 **Rethink your priorities and supporting goals** Decide on those things that you most want to achieve and set targeted, time-specific goals to help you achieve them.

12 **Stake your claim on a task or goal** The key to your success will be your ability to adopt tasks and goals as your own, whether they have been set by you or not.

13 **Aspire to be organized** When your work space is well organized, you have a better chance of being more efficient and productive.

14 **Manage your desk for decision** An uncluttered desk enables you to focus on the task in hand.

15 **Set up your work space for performance** Create a place where you can work to the best of your ability.

16   **Get your ducks in a row** Plan for your requirements before starting a project to avoid delays along the way.

17   **Live 'in the zone'** Identify and recreate the circumstances under which you do your best and most productive work.

18   **Decimate distractions** Devise strategies that enable you to start and complete tasks without interruption.

19   **Disconnect yourself** Cut yourself off mentally and physically to get the job done.

20   **Begin now, which is as good a time as any** The best time to start is right now.

NOTES

part
three

part
three

GIVE YOURSELF THE EDGE

SOLUTION 21
EXPLORE THE POWER OF SCENTS

*'He who loves the world as his body may be
entrusted with the empire.'*
Lao Tzu

In Solution 6, I introduced you to how you could
visualize success; now learn how you can smell your
way there. The sense of smell, more than any other, is
the quickest way to change your mood.

Studies have shown that specific scents can alter
our behaviour. The evidence is found in measurable
indicators of mood and emotion, such
as blood pressure, heart rate and
body temperature. By changing the
way we feel, aromas can enhance our
performance and our productivity.

*the scent of an orange
peel can make you feel
better about your day*

THE SCIENCE OF AROMATHERAPY

Aromatherapy works
by affecting the
neurological functioning
of the human body, and
smells travel faster than
your other senses to
the brain's limbic area,

Dentists have found that when they scent their
offices, patient resistance and fear seem to
diminish, right up until they hear the sound
of the dentist's drill. Even patients having root
canals, when immersed in a room primed
with relaxing scents, exhibited less anxiety
and higher levels of relaxation than those
in unscented rooms, and they reported pain
sensations less frequently.

where learning, memory and emotion are controlled. There are those who question the validity of aromatherapy and contend that the effects are psychological. In other words, they claim that people feel better simply because they believe that essential oils have therapeutic effects. But if it makes you feel better, does it matter how it works?

aromatherapy
use of essential oils and herbs to treat specific health- and stress-related conditions

QUICK FIX: MOOD CHANGERS

There are more than 300 essential oils, and they can affect you in different ways. If you would like to experiment, the following list will help you to get started:

Effect	Essential Oil
Antidepressants	Bergamot, geranium, lavender, patchouli, rosebuds, rosemary, sandalwood, St John's wort, ylang-ylang
Courage	Cedar, musk, rose, geranium
Harmony	Basil, gardenia, lilac, narcissus
Insomnia	Lavender, narcissus
Peace	Benzoin, cumin, gardenia, hyacinth, magnolia, rose, tuberose
Relaxation	Camomile, catnip, frankincense, hops, lavender, rosebuds
Stimulants	Lavender, lemon verbena, patchouli, peppermint, rosemary

SOLUTION 22
TUNE IN TO MOTIVATING MESSAGES

'The longest drought will end in rain.'
Robert Frost

It is a fact that we spend a large proportion of our life at work and not an inconsiderable amount of time getting there. In fact, one in five people takes at least an hour to get to work. Whether you travel by car or by train or even by foot, you can make the most of this time to re-energize your mind by taking the opportunity to listen to inspirational stories and motivational speakers. All you need is a CD or tape player or a MP3 player. Who knows, you may experience your very own Eureka moment on the way.

*make your journey
to work a worthwhile
experience*

COMMUTER LEARNING

Although commuting can often be exhausting and stressful, there is a way to transform it into a positive experience and make it more worthwhile. The average commuter spends about 139 hours a year travelling to and from work, and that is time that could be put to good use learning a language, listening to classic literature, or learning lessons in good business practice. Choose to listen to audio books that will prompt and inspire you to take action. The beauty of such listening experiences is that you get to pick what you want to hear, you make the most of your travel time, and there are no quizzes or end-of-term exams to worry about.

MUSIC FOR STRESS RELIEF

If things are getting on top of you at work, listening to music can really help to relieve the stress. Research has found that when we listen to music the depth of our breathing increases, which provides more oxygen and therefore more energy to the body. Also, serotonin is secreted in the brain, which acts as a mood stabilizer and can increase our overall feeling of well-being. Listening to music before bed can result in a sounder sleep, which is so important for our productivity (see Solution 37).

So the next time you're feeling uptight, stressed or anxious, tune in to music using these simple tips:

Listen to music you like Research has proven that listening to music that you dislike can raise your stress levels.

Go for variety Listening to the same song over and over again will lessen the music's stress-relieving effect.

Be considerate to others Put on headphones to avoid disturbing anyone else.

Listen as you walk Invest in an MP3 player and pop in your earphones to experience the additional benefits of fresh air and exercise.

Take 20 Listening for a minimum of 20 minutes can achieve the best result.

QUICK FIX: AUDIO INSPIRATIONS

The internet is the quickest way to access a library of inspirational lectures, motivational programs and interesting books of all sorts, as CDs, cassettes or downloads. Try *www.audible.co.uk* or *www.talkingbooks.co.uk*. Alternatively, visit your local library.

SOLUTION 23
UNSHACKLE YOURSELF FROM TOO MUCH INFORMATION

'The art of being wise is the art of knowing what to overlook.'
William James

Many people believe they need reams of data before making a decision, and so they put off making a decision at all. But in a society that deluges us with data, more data is not always the answer.

Enough data exists to lead to all possible answers, and this can get in the way of making a choice. More data does not necessarily produce a better answer, so don't let data overload stop you from making a decision. Change your relationship to information and learn to have faith in your instinctive choices.

too much information can get in the way of making clear-cut decisions

The US Secretary of State, Colin Powell, when interviewed in a *Time* magazine article following the Persian Gulf War, explained one of the reasons he had been able to make effective decisions in his military career. He would wait until he had about 60 per cent of the data that he could amass for a decision; then, rather than wait for all the 'hard' information to come in, he would make his choice based on the data he had, his experience and gut instinct.

INSTINCTIVE DECISIONS

A study on the use of information in making decisions took two groups of individuals who had to make purchase decisions. One group was given data, analysis and articles on which to base their decisions; the other group made their decisions based on instinct. The results were reviewed after a few weeks, and it was found that the group who had chosen on instinct felt better about their decisions.

instinct is not based on a moment's whim; it's everything you have ever learned to date

If you are a 40-year-old, 40 years of data is brought to bear when you make a decision. Each of us has the ability to make intuitive choices, but for many, the words 'intuition' and 'instinct' are taboo – yet the top CEOs of large companies often make decisions based on what feels right. Give yourself the opportunity to get started on projects more quickly by relying more on your internal decision-making.

QUICK FIX: CORE INFORMATION

When you receive a large packet of information, break it down to the few pages that you might need. Use the edge of a ruler to neatly tear out only the bits useful to you from each page. Assemble the selection on the copier and create a one- or two-page composite. This allows you to review the important information quickly at a later date, and keeps your files leaner and more targeted.

SOLUTION 24
ASK YOURSELF, 'WILL IT GET ANY EASIER LATER?'

'The doors we open and close each day decide the lives we live.'
Flora Whittemore

When faced with a task or project that you would rather put off, ask yourself this question: 'Will it be any easier later?' Most often, the answer is no.

Even minor tasks mount up. Each one then becomes a greater burden than if you had simply handled it as it arrived. If it will not be any easier to handle a task later, the easiest time to do it may well be now. 'Later' demands that you reacquaint yourself with the task, which in itself requires mental energy. And do you really have any of that to spare?

a stitch in time saves ninety-nine

NOW OR LATER?

Is there a letter or email that you need to respond to, or a phone call you should make? Will it be any easier or ultimately more beneficial to deal with it later? If the answer is no, handle it now.

Do not be tempted to park all those small jobs somewhere, intending to return to them later when you have more time, or you are in a better frame of mind to take them on. You know the chances are that you will never have more time and your mood may not improve either.

QUICK FIX: DO IT NOW

If you have been asked to do a small administrative task, such as filling in a professional survey, ask yourself the question, 'Will it be any easier to complete later?' If the answer is no, then do it now. The benefits of taking immediate action for minor tasks include:

- You don't have to remember to do it later.
- You won't park it only to discover it later (usually the day before or after its due date).
- It does not contribute to a pile of other uncompleted minor tasks.
- It never makes your 'to-do list', hence saving time.
- A quick, on-the-spot completion makes you feel productive.
- You enhance your reputation as someone who takes action quickly.
- You can reward yourself for one job done.

SOLUTION 25
FIND A FRIEND

'A problem shared is a problem halved.'
Proverb

If you are finding it difficult to get started on a project, accept that you may need help. Pairing up with a short-term partner can be of great advantage to you both. (See Solution 44 for long-term partnerships.)

Is there somebody trying to accomplish the same task and who, too, is experiencing similar roadblocks? If so, you may have found the perfect person to join forces with.

some tasks are simply too challenging to face alone

THE BENEFITS OF AFFILIATION

Finding yourself a partner, associate, collaborator, helpmate (or whatever you choose to call them) can have all sorts of benefits. Here are just a few:

An antidote to loneliness It is often easier to get started when you are working with a team member.

Safety in numbers Those tasks with highly unpredictable results are much more difficult to get underway, but sharing the challenge with a co-worker can spur you on.

A sounding board When you have an affiliate with whom you can share insights and to whom you can pose questions, you are less likely to find yourself stuck.

Enhanced chance of success When you team up with a colleague who's facing similar struggles, you have a greater chance of achieving your goal.

Support when things go wrong You can be sure of a sympathetic ally to share your problems with.

networking
developing personal contacts for exchange of information to further your career

A GUIDING HAND

Sometimes, all you may need is a guiding hand. If your ignorance on a subject is holding you back, or you lack the confidence to begin, find someone at your workplace or within the organization who has the knowledge or experience you need. Ask her to spend 10 minutes with you to answer any questions you may have. This may be just what you need to keep on track with your task.

QUICK FIX: NETWORKING OPPORTUNITIES

Seek out networking opportunities, as the people you meet today may help you to succeed tomorrow:

- Attend conferences or conventions populated with others in your industry.
- Collect the business cards and email addresses of people in other divisions of your own organization, or in entirely different organizations, who have responsibilities and challenges similar to your own.
- Get involved with groups or societies – commissions, ruling councils, unions, advisory boards, committees, councils, task forces – as they can often be a source of valuable allies.

SOLUTION 26
DON'T DELAY BECAUSE YOU'RE NOT 'IN THE MOOD'

'We are what we repeatedly do. Excellence, then, is not an act, but a habit.'
Aristotle

Many people believe that if they could only initiate tasks at the 'right time', then it would be easier to begin and complete them. But for most tasks, there is no 'right' time. Waiting until you are 'in the mood' for work is a waste of time and a poor excuse for not getting started on the job at hand.

in affairs of the heart, being 'in the mood' can make all the difference, but it has no place at work

The reality of today's business world is that waiting until one is 'in the mood' is a luxury that most people cannot afford; true professionals need to carry on regardless of how they feel.

In Hollywood's heyday, film stars who weren't 'in the mood' were given substantial leeway as they stormed off the set (one only has to think of the career of Marilyn Monroe). Today, however, such instances are rarely heard of. The film industry is highly competitive, budgets are tight, shooting schedules are meticulously planned well in advance, and investors expect compensatory returns for their risk. Actors are expected to perform on cue – there is no room for drama queens.

IMAGINE IF ...

Across society, from presidents to postal workers,
professionals have to carry on regardless of how they
feel. The difference between a professional
writer and an amateur one is that the
professional writes to schedule whether he is
in the mood or not. Imagine a psychologist,
with a full day's schedule, telling her clients,
'I don't feel like going ahead with our
appointment right now'; or a professional
boxer, in the middle of a bout, dropping his guard, and
saying, 'I'm just not in the mood.'

*taking action usually
proves to be so
invigorating that your
mood will positively
change anyway*

WHAT ABOUT YOU?

Just like any other professional, you have to perform,
often on cue, regardless of how you feel at any
particular moment. Under deadline at the office, it
makes no difference whether you're in the mood to
handle a job or not. No doubt you accomplish great
things everyday when at the outset you weren't in the
mood; just muster the impetus to start and you'll do fine.
Once you begin, whether or not you are in the mood
will become irrelevant.

SOLUTION 27
JUMP-START A PROJECT

*'Let him who would enjoy a good future
waste none of his present.'*
Roger Babson

Often all you need is a jump-start to get you started
on that task you have been putting off. Simply turning
on your computer, popping a disk into the CD player,
or flipping on your pocket recorder may be enough to
get you going. Just like a car that has a
run-down battery, once you have jump-
started yourself into action and have
the engine revving, you will want to keep
going for a good 20 minutes.

*find some element of
the task that you
can complete quickly
and easily*

THE EXTRA BENEFIT

Sometimes, it doesn't get much easier than pushing
the power button. The sound of your computer
booting up may be all you need to motivate you to
begin. And, as an extra bonus, jump-starting yourself
in this way often enables you to capture your first, and
sometimes best, thoughts. Jump-starting can often
be facilitated by giving your task a preview, so read
through Solution 28.

BRING IN THE MECHANIC

If, to take on a new project, you find that you have to learn a new software program or master some new piece of equipment, and you are dreading it, this may be the only excuse you need to put off getting started. When you are stalled because you don't have the technological knowledge, it's time to get some help (see Solution 25). Tackle just what you need to know, and rather than becoming enmeshed in all the features of a new software program, focus instead on mastering only the handful of capabilities you may need.

find a trusted guide to help you to deal with those frustrating tasks you may encounter

QUICK FIX: BREAKING THROUGH THE 'GEEK SPEAK'

There is no point spending endless hours in front of your computer, with the software instruction manual in hand, starting and stopping, presuming that you can suddenly become adept at skills for which you have previously shown no aptitude. Find someone who can help you to navigate a way through and establish sequences and routines that you can follow easily. Concentrate on the 'what if' questions to find the route that best suits you:

• What if I wanted to do this?
• What if I wanted to combine that?
• What if I wanted to eliminate this?

SOLUTION 28
PREVIEW YOUR TASK

'I owe all my success in life to having always been a quarter of an hour beforehand.'
Horatio Nelson

If you are on a countdown to starting a project that you are not looking forward to, it can help if you take the time to preview your task.

Say, for example, you have a major project to begin first thing on Monday morning. An effective manoeuvre is to invest just a little time on Friday afternoon to briefly review the assignment before you go home. Then forget about it for the weekend. When you turn up for

a few minutes spent last thing on Friday can prove invaluable in facilitating Monday-morning tasks

A fellow speaker who had heard me lecture on previewing tasks emailed me to recount her own preview success story. Waking in the middle of the night and unable to get back to sleep, she recalled my presentation. Grabbing the folder of a project she would be working on later that morning, she reviewed its contents while she lay awake. After a while, she drifted back to sleep. In the morning, when she reopened the project folder, she was pleasantly surprised at the ease with which she began working. Her late-night preview served as an effective jump-start for her morning task (see Solution 27).

work on the Monday, you will find that it
is much easier to get started than you
had anticipated.

SO HOW DOES IT WORK?

Spending even just 10 minutes previewing next
week's tasks can prove invaluable. You might look over
supporting documents, jot down some notes, or begin
a rough outline, and your ideas and thoughts can flow
freely during this period while it 'doesn't count'. Over the
weekend, your subconscious gets started on the project,
germinating ideas or letting a plan develop. Come
Monday morning, when it does count, you will be ready
to tackle the project head-on, and your stress load will
be cut by half.

QUICK FIX: EFFECTIVE PREVIEWING

The early preview is the key to the success of this technique.
Try previewing:

- Monday-morning tasks on Friday afternoon
- Post-holiday tasks before you go on holiday
- Afternoon tasks before you go out to lunch
- End-of-week tasks during the middle of the week
- Any task either a few days or hours before working on it

SOLUTION 29
RECOGNIZE THAT WANTING IS DIFFERENT FROM DECIDING

'In the depths of winter I finally learned there was in me an invincible summer.'
Albert Camus

It is often very difficult to get started on a project that you quite simply don't want to work on, now or ever. But just like the professional who doesn't wait until he is in the mood to do a job (see Solution 26), your preference for a project has nothing to do with your decision to get started on it.

Deciding or *choosing* to start on a project is quite different from *wanting* to start on a project.

if you have an important project due, forget about whether or not you want to start it and simply decide to begin

IT'S ONLY WORDS

This, you may say, is merely a matter of semantics. How can playing with words help you break through procrastination? Well, you learned in Solution 8 how a change in language could make all the difference to how you approach a particular project. What you 'should' do is not nearly as invigorating as something you will 'be happy' to do. Likewise, 'choosing to' or 'deciding to' start on a project liberates you when you don't particularly 'fancy' doing it.

SOLUTION 30
TAKE ON THE HARD STUFF FIRST

'Hard work is often the easy work you did not do at the proper time.'
Bernard Meltzer

If you can control the order in which you tackle the steps on the way to achieving your task, it can pay to get the things that you are least looking forward to out of the way first, and that's usually the hard things.

If you do the things you like first and save the unpleasant or difficult things for last, procrastination may set in, preventing you from successfully completing the task. When you handle the unpleasant tasks first, you are less likely to put off completing the project and your chances of success are greatly improved.

get the difficult things under your belt first and save the sweet stuff till last

SUMMARY: PART THREE
GIVE YOURSELF THE EDGE

21   **Explore the power of scents** Experiment with essential oils to discover how aromas can enhance your performance and productivity.

22   **Tune in to motivating messages** Make the most of your commuting time to re-energize your mind by listening to inspirational stories and motivational speakers.

23   **Unshackle yourself from too much information** Too much data can get in the way of making clear-cut decisions; learn to have faith in your instinctive choices.

24   **Ask yourself, 'Will it get any easier later?'** Discover the benefits of taking immediate action for those minor tasks.

25   **Find a friend** Teaming up with a partner can help you deal with a challenging project.

26 Don't delay because you're not 'in the mood' True professionals need to carry on regardless of how they feel.

27 Jump-start a project Turn on your computer now and get ready to capture your first – which are often your best – thoughts.

28 Preview your task To facilitate Monday-morning jobs, set aside a little time on Friday afternoon to review the assignment before you go home for the weekend.

29 Recognize that wanting is different from deciding If you have an important project due, forget about whether or not you want to start it and simply decide to begin.

30 Take on the hard stuff first Get the difficult tasks ticked off first and save the sweet stuff till last.

NOTES

part
four

part
four

COME OUT CHARGING

SOLUTION 31
MAKE A CHOICE – CHOOSE SUCCESS

'Procrastination becomes less likely on tasks that we openly and freely choose to undertake.'
Steve Pavlina

There is little power in choosing by avoidance, but there is great power in directly addressing what you want. If you choose to do something, you are more likely to be successful in seeing it through to a conclusion.

By continuing to make positive choices, you are in control of how you feel, act and perform, rather than reacting and responding to the actions of others. By acknowledging your present emotions – whether you are angry, anxious, elated or sad – you release blocked energy and begin to live in the present. The choices you make today will affect your behaviour and performance.

you are in control of your progress and how your day unfolds

Robert Fritz, founder of Technologies for Creating, teaches that by making choices and positive affirmations regarding what you want, you move closer each day to realizing what you want to accomplish. Making deeply pronounced choices is an effective way to overcome procrastination. The choices you make, Fritz suggests, are best made regularly, regardless of how you feel at the moment you make them.

QUICK FIX: POSITIVE CHOICES

Below are a few examples of the positive choices you can make to motivate yourself to achieve your goals. When formulating choices of your own, take care to word them to indicate what you want rather than what you wish to avoid; for example, 'I choose to easily get started on the task at hand,' rather than 'I hope I don't get delayed beginning this project.'

I choose to:

- easily get started on the task at hand
- enjoy my work
- acknowledge my accomplishments each day
- make steady progress
- maintain balance and harmony
- remain organized and in control
- feel comfortable in the face of uncertainty
- approach my task with enthusiasm
- decisively handle the challenges I face
- maintain high productivity all day
- build momentum towards my goals
- form powerful partnerships with colleagues
- leave work feeling energized
- make new choices as needed

SOLUTION 32
ALLOW TIME FOR REFLECTION

*'Men give me credit for some genius. All the genius
I have lies in this: When I have a subject in hand
I study it profoundly.'*
Alexander Hamilton

One of the biggest obstacles to consistent productivity is the unwillingness most people have to take short breaks during their working day. Everyone needs a few moments for quiet reflection. By taking just a little time to pause for contemplation, the tasks and projects you face each day can seem less daunting.

*looking out the window
could be the single
most important and
productive thing you
do today*

Has the following ever happened to you? Somebody walks by your desk while you are reading and gives you a funny look. You start to feel guilty that you are not doing something more active and you worry that your workmates will think that you are procrastinating. Yet consider that studies reveal that informed people in executive positions read for 2 to 4 hours each day. To be as creative, you must give yourself permission to act in ways that run counter to what society tells you are 'productive'.

THE BENEFITS OF REFLECTION

If, like many other business people today, you feel perpetually overwhelmed, you need to learn the value of taking regular breaks throughout your day. By engaging in appropriate, reliable ways to find solace and inner guidance both at home and work, you can reduce your stress levels and this will enable you to face challenges in your career and personal life more effectively.

As well as taking the time for quiet reflection, you should resist the temptation to be seen to be doing something active. When we're each continually encountering messages that exalt motion and activity, merely reflecting for a moment, or reading or thinking, doesn't seem to be worthwhile, yet these activities should not be undervalued.

sometimes the best way to be productive is to be doing nothing, or at least nothing that looks like anything to people walking by

QUICK FIX: TAKE A BREAK

Sometimes the best way to be productive is to be doing nothing, or at least nothing that looks like anything to people walking by. Break out of the 'in motion' mindset and make time during your working day to read, to stare out the window, or to just 'take a minute' a couple of times each day. To put yourself into pause mode quickly, try looking at your watch for 60 seconds.

SOLUTION 33
REWARD YOURSELF

*'Go confidently in the direction of your dreams.
Live the life you have imagined.'*
Henry David Thoreau

It's a well-known fact that positively reinforced behaviour gets repeated. If you reward yourself for accomplishing the small tasks on the way to your goal, you'll have a greater chance of being successful.

In his book *Bringing Out the Best in People*, Aubrey Daniels, PhD, discusses the concept of scheduling a reward following a good performance, known by some as the 'Grandma principle'. As Grandma would say, you don't get your ice cream until you eat your spinach! If you're facing an unpleasant task, it makes sense to follow it up with something you enjoy doing. In other words, you don't get to do what you enjoy until you complete the unpleasant task.

QUICK FIX: JUST REWARDS

Incentivize yourself to complete those jobs that you are not looking forward to by rewarding yourself on their completion. Rewards will vary according to your personal tastes, but here are a few ideas:

- Call or email a friend.
- Take a 20-minute walk.
- Log on to your favourite website.
- Watch a television show.
- Read a magazine or a chapter from a book.
- Have a lie-in.
- Do a crossword puzzle.
- Do whatever tickles your fancy.

SOLUTION 34
MAKE A CONTRACT WITH YOURSELF

'Whether you believe you can do a thing or not, you are right.'
Henry Ford

Feature writer and author Dennis Hensley describes what he calls 'Advancement by Contract'. He

a contract takes precedence over everything else

suggests carefully selecting three to five major activities in support of some task you want to accomplish and then signing a contract *with yourself* to aid you in completing your goals. A sample contract is provided here for you.

Make three copies of your contract, and give them to your partner, a work colleague and a friend. Review your contract when you find yourself becoming distracted by small details. (For a more stringent approach along the same theme, see Solution 49.)

SELF-INITIATED CONTRACT

I, ..., agree to accomplish each of the following items on or before .... and hereby do formally contract myself to these purposes. These items are challenging, but reasonable, and I accept them willingly.

1...

2...

3...

Signature .... Date ....

SOLUTION 35
PRODUCE A PLAN

'The future belongs to those who believe in the beauty of their dreams.'
Eleanor Roosevelt

When it comes to initiating a task or project, it can be difficult to motivate yourself to begin if you lack either a clear starting point or a logical sequence of steps to take. You are more likely to be successful if you take the time to outline a succinct plan of action.

When you plot your course, suddenly the task seems easier. You have a direction to follow and a focus for your energies. Develop the patience to make a plan and the discipline to stick to it.

make a simple plan no longer than the length of a Post-it pad

When best-selling novelist John Grisham begins one of his legal thrillers, he charts a course of action on a scale most people would never attempt. Producing a comprehensive outline for each chapter, his novel outlines range from 60 to 80 pages long. When he begins writing the book's narrative, at no point is he ever lost, as he can refer to this document for exactly what to write next. If such a grand plan can lead to Grisham's spectacular success, think what just a simple plan can do for you.

FIRST STEPS TO PLANNING

Always write down your plan of action. Once your course is 'out of your head' and 'on the page', you free up your mental energy to focus on each step.

Plot a course Sketch out the five, seven, nine, or however many steps required to accomplish the deed.

Take a step at a time List these key words or phrases in progression, in the order in which you believe you need to do them at the project's outset.

Assess progress every couple of steps Review your plan often; it may be necessary to revise the plan as you become more aware of the realities of your task; for example, you may need to reorder the steps or add new steps.

Determine that you're on the right course If the plan isn't working, don't be afraid to replan.

Measure your progress Use the plan to keep track of your accomplishments as you work towards completion.

QUICK FIX: PLANNING

If you need help tackling large tasks, consider investing in a software program such as Above & Beyond (*www.1soft.com*), which helps you to split large projects into definable tasks and generate reports and invoices.

SOLUTION 36
BARGAIN WITH YOURSELF

'Right now is the most important moment in your life.'
Robert Fritz

One way to keep yourself motivated at work is to assess what you've accomplished (and what more you want to accomplish) from time to time throughout the day, adjusting to new conditions as they emerge. I call this dynamic bargaining.

The dynamic bargain is a self-reinforcing tool for achieving a desired outcome, identified by you, within a certain time frame.

end your day feeling good about what you have accomplished

FEELING FULFILLED AND FULFILLING YOUR JOB

Ask yourself, 'What would it take for me to feel good about ending work on time today?' Suppose that on any given day, your answer to the question is to finish three particular items on your desk.

Now imagine that your boss drops a project on your desk late in the day. Don't panic; just strike a new dynamic bargain with yourself. Adapting to the new circumstances, your bargain might be to make sufficient headway on this new project, or to accomplish two of your previous three tasks and 'x' per cent of the new task.

MAKE THE MOST OF EVERY MINUTE

Your ability to strike dynamic bargains with yourself, and to rebargain as circumstances change, will help you to overcome the all-too-common tendency to dawdle as the end of a time interval approaches, such as before lunch or at the end of the day. The restriking of dynamic bargains will help you to overcome any intrusions – late projects, email, phone calls – and enable you to remain productive all day long.

dynamic bargain an agreement you make with yourself to assess your progress, adjusting to new conditions as they emerge

SOLUTION 37
REST WELL AND EAT HEALTHILY

'A problem difficult at night is resolved in the morning after the committee of sleep has worked on it.'
John Steinbeck

When you are well rested and well nourished, you have the best chance of doing your best work. When you are not getting enough sleep and your diet is poor, even the smallest tasks can seem more difficult than they are. When you are tackling a challenging project it is even more important to rest well and eat healthily.

a good night's sleep makes you better able to tackle life's challenges

ARE YOU GETTING ENOUGH SLEEP?

If you are having trouble getting started, it may be your body's way of telling you that you need to put a little relaxation back into your life. Some experts believe that getting too little sleep on a consistent basis may undermine your entire being. You are more likely to succumb to colds and viruses, and any illness that you do contract will be more severe. Here's a list of indicators that show you may not be getting sufficient sleep:

- Your eyes are red, and colleagues keep telling you how tired you look.
- You are not mentally sharp.
- You avoid tasks that involve adding up numbers.
- You often find yourself daydreaming.
- When interacting with others you simply go through the motions.
- You avoid taking telephone calls if you can.
- You watch the clock throughout the day, hoping the time will go by more quickly.

GETTING THE RIGHT TYPE OF SLEEP

Deep rapid eye movement (REM) sleep enables you to more fully engage in conceptual, first-time and breakthrough thinking. If you have to learn a new routine, new instructions or new equipment, the amount and quality of REM sleep you get the night before is very important. If your REM pattern is disrupted, even 8 hours of sleep may not yield the benefits you need to be effective.

QUICK FIX: ENERGY BOOSTERS

The periods of highest alertness for most people are between 9am and noon, and 4pm and 8pm. So how do you keep yourself going throughout a normal 8-hour working day? Here are some ideas:
- Spray your office with an energizing aroma (see Solution 21).
- Go for a power walk at lunchtime.
- Replace a chocolate-bar snack with a banana or an oatcake.
- Take an energy-boosting supplement such as ginseng.
- Drink plenty of water (about 2 litres) each day.

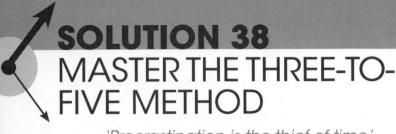

SOLUTION 38
MASTER THE THREE-TO-FIVE METHOD

'Procrastination is the thief of time.'
Edward Young

Whenever you start work on a new project, it can help to identify a part of the task that you can complete quickly and easily. This immediate 'win' will spur you on, and is often a far easier method of getting started than tackling the most difficult parts first. If you can tackle several small tasks, all the better.

> *identify three to five things you could do to progress towards the final objective without actually tackling a project head-on*

EASY WINS

The three-to-five'method espoused by time management guru Alan Lakein asks that you initiate those 'easy entry' activities first. For example, suppose you are facing a difficult project; identify an easy win. Open up the file folder, scan through the contents, and look for something that's familiar to you; often this represents an easy entry point.

Sometimes simply organizing materials, putting them into smaller file folders, stapling items, bookmarking websites or rearranging the order of things represent good, early wins. Now at least you will have a better handle on the project, the supporting items will be arranged in their order of importance, and you can be reasonably sure that you'll continue on your course of action.

THE THREE-TO-FIVE METHOD IN ACTION

Suppose you've been putting off some task assigned to you, such as moving files into storage. It would seem relatively straightforward: you either move the files or not. But if it were that simple, you would have moved them ages ago. By employing the three-to-five method, you can motivate yourself to get started, and in this scenario, five entry activities might be:

One Obtain the trolley you'll need to haul the contents away.
Two Roll up your sleeves.
Three Sift through the items to survey the scope of work.
Four Divide up the documents into quarters and tackle one on Monday morning, one on Monday afternoon, one on Tuesday before midday, and one on Tuesday evening.
Five Recruit a colleague to assist you on Monday afternoon and Tuesday evening when your own energy levels are likely to be flagging.

SOLUTION 39
SUM UP THE COSTS OF PROCRASTINATION

'The problem is not that there are problems. The problem is expecting otherwise and thinking that having problems is a problem.'
Theodore Rubin

If you find it difficult to get motivated, try asking yourself what your procrastination costs you. Procrastination can affect your health, your personal life and your career development. Realizing what you have to lose may spur you to get going. Write these headings on a piece of paper: physical, monetary, mental, professional, social. Here are a few things to consider:

Physical costs Sleepless nights, anxiety attacks, headaches and psychological stress.
Monetary costs Pounds lost, from nothing to hundreds, or even thousands; affect on bonus or raise; career and business opportunities at stake.
Mental costs Damage to your self-worth; knock to your self-confidence; affect on your personal relationships.
Professional costs Your professional reputation; your chances of receiving a promotion.
Social costs All those invitations rejected when fretting about put-off tasks; missed opportunities for meeting new friends or significant others.

SOLUTION 40
COUNT TO FOUR

'Heroism consists in hanging on a minute longer.'
Norwegian proverb

If you're having a hard time getting started on a task, and you really *do* need to get started, make a promise to yourself that you'll do it, but just for 4 minutes. After those first 4 minutes, you will have the option of stopping or continuing as you choose. Fortunately, more often than not, you will find that you want to keep on going.

*a David-sized tip with a
Goliath-sized pay-off*

WHY DOES IT WORK?

The 4-minute approach is a bit like dangling your feet in a pool. Before you know it, you're swimming lengths.

Most people who use the 4-minute approach don't want to stop after the fourth minute. They gain an impetus and can begin to see the way forward; in short, they become engaged in the task. After spending 4 minutes on the task, there is no reason why the fifth, sixth or seventh minute will be any more trying.

SUMMARY: PART FOUR
COME OUT CHARGING

31   **Make a choice – choose success** If you choose to do something, you are more likely to be successful in seeing it through to its conclusion.

32   **Allow time for reflection** Taking regular breaks throughout the working day can make you more productive.

33   **Reward yourself** Incentivize yourself to complete those jobs that you are not looking forward to by rewarding yourself on their completion.

34   **Make a contract with yourself** The self-initiated contract will help you keep on track to achieving your goals.

35   **Produce a plan** Once your course of action is down on paper, you are set free to focus on each step.

36 Bargain with yourself Continuously review what you would like to achieve so that you can end the day feeling good about what you have accomplished.

37 Rest well and eat healthily When you are well rested and well nourished, you have the best chance of doing your best work.

38 Master the three-to-five method When getting underway with a project, identify and achieve the quick wins.

39 Sum up the costs of procrastination Realizing what you've got to lose may be just what you need to get you started on a task.

40 Count to four Work on your task for at least 4 minutes and the chances are you will want to carry on once that time is up.

NOTES

part
five

part
five

TAKE ON THE HARDER TASKS

SOLUTION 41
STAY FIT; KEEP IT FUN

'Do not let circumstances control you.
You change your circumstances.'
Jackie Chan

Have you put off exercising . . . for weeks, months or even years? The people of industrialized nations around the world are battling weight problems and obesity unlike any generation before. With so many demands on our time, it is all too easy to come up with excuses not to exercise. Yet staying fit can reap benefits in both your working and personal life.

reap the benefits of engaging in a regular programme of exercise

MOTIVATE YOURSELF TO EXERCISE – A LEARNING EXPERIENCE

When you get in from work, don't give in to the temptation to slump in front of the television – jump instead! Combine a home workout session with a learning experience. An ultra-effective method to stay fit is to make your exercise sessions learning experiences too. Record or rent interesting series on topics that interest you – science, history, geography, the arts and so on.

By exercising at the same time as watching television, you can avoid the tendency most people have to eat while viewing, and, at the same time, you can be adding to your storehouse of knowledge.

NO EXCUSES NOW

If you have been putting off exercise for years, you are probably making up excuses right at this minute for why this system won't work for you.

'The kids are watching the TV' Most homes have more than one television, but even if yours doesn't, you can download lots of interesting programmes on your computer with BBC iPlayer, ITV player and 4oD.

'I need some down time' Watch and exercise for 20 minutes, press pause, take a shower, then come back to watch the rest of the programme.

'I get in too late; there just isn't the time' Get up an hour earlier at the beginning of the day and do your viewing before everyone else is up.

'I don't have anything to watch' Log on to *www.lovefilm.com*. Alternatively, try your local library or ask your family and friends if they would like to swap series.

QUICK FIX: STAYING FIT

When you are really busy at work, often exercise is one of the first things to fall off your to-do list. Here are three quick ideas to squeeze exercise into even the busiest of days:

- Park in the farthest spot in the garage or car park.
- Use the stairs instead of taking the lift.
- Take a 5- to 10-minute walk after lunch.

SOLUTION 42
DIVE RIGHT IN

'I ain't wasting time no more, 'cause time goes by like hurricanes and faster things.'
Gregg Allman

Sometimes the best way to get started on a task is to dive right in and get it over with.

If you can recall a recent trip to the swimming pool, no doubt there was at least one person standing shivering on the side of the pool in endless turmoil about the best way to get in. Should they jump, climb down the ladder, or sit on the side to get acclimatized to the water first? What they needed was a good shove – after a few seconds they'd have been wondering what they had made such a fuss about.

you might even wonder why you spent so much time getting started

So, too, when taking on a new project, you may need to immerse yourself in the task without thinking about it for too long. It may not be anywhere as bad as you fear; in fact, it can be a great relief. This solution, though not recommended for everyone, or for every time, is sometimes the only way forward.

My friend Jim Cathcart, a fellow professional speaker, made the decision a few years back to throw out all of his hard-copy slides so that he would be forced to learn presentation software and convert his audio-visuals to newer, more powerful media.

SOLUTION 43
LISTEN TO YOURSELF

'If we don't change, we don't grow. If we don't grow, we aren't really living.'
Gail Sheehy

When you find yourself procrastinating, the following technique can help you to motivate yourself to begin. Speaking into a tape recorder, lay out the task or project, as you understand it; now outline the reason or reasons holding you back from getting started on it. Hours or even days later, replay your recording.

It may be difficult to hear in your own words the reasons you have given for your delay, but more often than not a breakthrough will occur and you will 'hear through' your own empty arguments. Before long, you will have had enough of your lame excuses, and you will be more than ready to make up for lost time.

In his book *Emotional Resilience,* David Viscott MD recounts how during counselling sessions he routinely recorded the responses of his patients when they were asked to describe their problems and the obstacles they believed to be in their way to overcoming them. When he replayed the tapes on subsequent visits, something extraordinary happened. Many patients found listening to the flimsy arguments they had been playing over and over again in their minds unbearable and were able to take steps to move on. Although it may have been hard to deal with their problems, it was harder to listen to their feeble reasons for not doing so.

SOLUTION 44
TEAM UP ON YOUR WAY TO ACHIEVEMENT

'Two are better than one . . . for if they fall, the one will lift up his fellow. But woe to him that is alone when he falleth, and hath not another to lift him up.'
Ecclesiastes 4:9–10

In Solution 25 you learned the value of affiliating with others facing the same task as you, and in Solution 27 of getting help from a knowledgeable colleague. It may be worth considering, therefore, if, for your long-term success, it would be mutually beneficial to find a partner who can help you get started and stay on course. There's something about working together that can spur people on to achieve great things way beyond their usual performance standards.

if you like your partner, that's gravy on your mashed potatoes

Composer Richard Rodgers and lyricist Oscar Hammerstein, better known as songwriting duo Rodgers and Hammerstein, were responsible for creating a string of popular Broadway musicals in the 1940s and 1950s including *Oklahoma!, Carousel, South Pacific, The King and I* and *The Sound of Music*. Together they achieved 34 Tony Awards, 15 Academy Awards, the Pulitzer Prize and two Grammys, and yet, despite their professional successes, they are said to have frequently feuded and rarely spoke to each other when not working. Hammerstein once said of Rodgers, 'I hand him a lyric and get out of his way.'

GREAT PARTNERSHIPS

From Laurel and Hardy to Lennon and
McCartney, a team of two can be a great
creative force. The synergy that some
teams muster is a marvel to behold. There's
something special about having one other
person with whom you collaborate, and it can often
bring out the best in both of you. So, who do you know
who could help you?

WHAT MAKES A GOOD PARTNERSHIP?

When looking for the perfect person to partner with,
it is important to remember that this is a professional
collaboration and not a personal friendship. As long as
one colleague respect the talents or contributions of the
other, a partnership can go on and on, independent of
what type of relationship the individuals have otherwise.
In other words, it is not compulsory to like each other, but
trust and communication are essential.

It is worth bearing in mind that it can give you a
head start to team up with someone who has already
had to tackle similar problems to those facing you.

SOLUTION 45
DELEGATE OR DIE

'The secret of success lies not in doing your own work but in recognizing the right person to do it.'
Andrew Carnegie

Where is it written that you have to personally handle each and every task necessary for the completion of a project? It is not shirking to find someone else who can effectively complete a task for you. If you allow yourself to believe that you alone can handle all tasks, your problems are just beginning.

Sometimes it makes sense to delegate those parts of a job that you don't have time to do yourself and that can just as easily be done by others. On other occasions you may find that you do not have the skill required to complete a task, so someone else would much better do it. The real skill lies in knowing what to delegate and what not to.

capitalize on your strengths and shore up your weaknesses by getting help

THE SKILLED WORK

Let's face it, there are some tasks that you're not going to do well, no matter how hard you try, how many lessons you take, or how long you practise. Some people will never excel at playing the piano, or be expert at computer programming, or shine at creative writing. If you want to 'nurture your nature', as author Jim Cathcart says in *The*

Acorn Principle, you need to capitalize on your strengths and shore up your weaknesses by getting help. Accept that there may be someone else in your company who can do the job more effectively than you.

THE SEED WORK

It can make sense to delegate the more routine aspects of a project. Many tasks are essential, but it is not essential that you do them. Indeed, some routine tasks can be quite bothersome and may be putting you off getting started at all. Delegating the everyday tasks frees up your time for other, possibly more important, tasks.

QUICK FIX: JOBS TO DELEGATE

What could others accomplish for you? Take a look:

- Serve routine customer needs.
- Make deliveries and pick-ups.
- Sort the post.
- Answer requests for information.
- Send out mailings of any sort.
- Make first-round or lead calls to prospective customers.
- Hunt for a product or service you need.
- Catalogue new information or products.
- Proofread copy.

- Survey customers and assess their needs.
- Keep track of necessary data and news sources.
- Type up mailing lists.
- Keep things tidy, clean and in good repair.
- Study competitors' literature and products.
- Track inventory or arrange displays.
- Collect breakfast or lunch.

SOLUTION 46
DO ONE THING AT A TIME

'Until you value yourself, you won't value your time. Until you value your time, you will not do anything with it.'
M. Scott Peck

The ability to juggle tasks is often seen as a strength. However, be warned: by continually switching back and forth between jobs, you may end up avoiding the one key task among the many that must be finished.

The single best way to deal with a number of different projects is to work on one thing until it is complete, then move on to the next, then the next, until all are done. For more on this, see Solution 56.

give yourself the benefit of working on one thing at a time

Switching between different projects can feel dynamic, but don't be fooled into thinking that multitasking is more productive. You can test this out quite easily with the help of a colleague. Decide on three minor tasks that both of you can engage in simultaneously, for example, stacking pennies, drawing 15 stars on a blank sheet of paper, and linking paperclips together. Sit opposite each other. You should indiscriminately alternate between tasks, while your colleague should complete each task before moving on to the next. By being able to focus on each task in turn, your workmate will finish before you and his work is likely to be of a better quality – his stacks of pennies are less likely to have toppled and his stars will be more consistent.

ASSESSING YOUR PROGRESS

Switching from task to task is not as productive as staying on one job until it is completed. To get the most out of the time you put in, it is important to keep focused on the task at hand. If staying on task seems onerous, periodically assessing your progress can help. For the multitude of projects you face, veering off course on one or many of them is an everyday phenomenon. It is for this very reason that continually switching between projects is so risky.

If you stay focused on the task at hand and periodically monitor your overall progress, you will be better able to deal with the necessary adjustments you may need to make to achieve the final goal successfully. If you keep bouncing back and forth between projects, you may fail to notice when things are going wrong, and by the time you do, you may not be able to get things back on course.

QUICK FIX: MANAGING YOUR IN-TRAY

The management of your in-tray is a classic example of the importance of maintaining focus. Always:

- Process the top item first.
- Deal with one item at a time.
- Never put anything back into 'in' – either delegate it, deal with it now, file it to review it at a later date, or throw it in the bin.

SOLUTION 47
APPLY THE HEAVY HALF MENTALITY

'Slow and steady wins the race.'
Aesop

When you engage in any task, you should always aim to go beyond the halfway point before taking a break. By taking care of the heavy half first, you will be more energized to complete the shorter, lighter second half.

It will take some discipline and rigour to proceed past the halfway point before stopping, but once you do, you may even find that you are motivated to continue till the job is finished.

when you are closer to your destination than to your point of origin, it is often easier to continue

When in the early 1970s, Mr Mott, a local businessman from West Hartford, Connecticut, needed his car in Florida, he would pay responsible college students like me to make the 27-hour drive for him. Flying in to Miami, he would meet the student, pay the agreed-upon fee, and provide a one-way airline ticket home. When making that long drive, my strategy was to never stop to sleep until well after the halfway point had been passed. When I woke the next day, I was always motivated to get going knowing that the final leg of my journey would be much shorter than the day before.

DEALING WITH THE HEAVY HALF LIGHTENS THE HEAVY HEART

Adopting the heavy half mentality works particularly well for those jobs that you find highly challenging. If you decide to take a break too soon, or if you are interrupted by other demands on your time, it can take you much longer to get started when returning to the project. You know that you will need to refamiliarize yourself with the task and that some repetition will be necessary, and this may put you off completing the job. However, if you are able to continue with a task until you are 55, 60 or, better still, 65 per cent of the way to completion, you will find it is much easier to finish quickly.

QUICK FIX: LIGHTEN THE LOAD

You can use the heavy half approach to lighten the load in all sorts of situations:

Writing a report You'll find the second shorter half will be much easier to complete.

Giving a long presentation The audience are likely to get less fidgety if you explain at the outset that the first half will be longer than the second.

Making a purchase on installment If you can, pay a little more on the first installment so you can pay a little less on the second one.

SOLUTION 48
EMPLOY THE BIGGER AND BADDER METHOD

'To avoid criticism, do nothing, say nothing and be nothing.'
Elbert Hubbard

If you are faced with two difficult tasks, and if one seems much worse than the other, you will find that it is easier to get started on the less difficult task, knowing that, by doing so, you are not having to work on the bigger, badder one.

By identifying and choosing to get started on the lesser of two evils, you have found an effective technique to counteract your procrastination.

if you continue to recognize bigger and badder tasks on the horizon, whatever difficult task you are currently facing will seem much more manageable

Your car insurance is up for renewal and your premiums have gone through the roof yet again. You know you need to find a cheaper insurer, or maybe even trade in your car for one that is cheaper to run, but you keep putting it off, as it is just too daunting to contemplate. Then, you receive your tax return … and suddenly the little matter of your car insurance renewal doesn't seem so big or so bad after all. You make a trade-off with yourself that you will put the tax return on hold until you have dealt with the car insurance.

THE TRADE-OFF

You can harness your procrastination to create energy for handling the tasks before you. Let's say you've got project A but you have been putting it off for weeks. When the more difficult project B is assigned to you, you have a big incentive to make project B what you're procrastinating about and to get to work on project A. When project A is complete, project B is what you are delaying getting started on, until of course project C comes along.

If you can continue to recognize bigger and badder tasks on the horizon, whatever difficult task you are currently facing will seem much more manageable.

TIME SHIFTING

Some time-management experts would criticize substituting one activity for another as procrastination, but I prefer to think of it as time shifting. So, you are taking on troublesome project A just because you would rather not deal with the even more onerous project B, but there is no doubt that project A does need to be done and that you will be much better off once it is completed. You will begin on project B eventually once you identify the even harder project C, as then project B will seem a lot easier to achieve.

SOLUTION 49
ESTABLISH AN ESCROW

'Time is money.'
Benjamin Franklin

This is an extreme, yet powerful, technique for those who are desperate to overcome their struggle with procrastination. It involves placing a significant sum of money – as determined by you – in the safekeeping of another until you manage to complete a specified project you have been avoiding. If you fail to finish the job within the time limit you have set yourself, the sum is forfeited to the person who is looking after it. (For a less drastic version of this technique, see Solution 34.)

To safeguard the disbursement of such funds should you fail to complete the agreed-upon task, consider instructing the person who holds the sum to donate it to a favourite charity. Alternatively, make the escrow holder the beneficiary and choose someone who, though trustworthy, least deserves to benefit from your failure; this may be all the incentive you require to fulfil your goal

IT'S A GAMBLE

The key to the effectiveness of this method is ensuring that the reserved sum is significant to you. It might be £50 or £500, but it should be enough that you will feel its loss. If this technique does not work for you after a second go, abandon the strategy before you go bankrupt.

escrow
a fund held
in reserve

SOLUTION 50
SEEK COUNSELLING

'Forget regret, or life is yours to miss.'
Jonathan Larson

If there is a chance that your lack of motivation and your tendency for procrastination have deep-rooted causes, and if you have exhausted all other avenues of support – friends, associates, relatives, supervisors and mentors – it may be time to seek help from a professional counsellor or psychotherapist.

counselling
working with a variety of individuals and their everyday problems in individual, family, or group settings

WHICH THERAPY?

Talking to someone confidentially who is not a friend or family member can make all the difference. Psychological therapies generally fall into three categories that are broadly described as:

Behavioural therapies These focus on cognitions and behaviours.
Psychoanalytical and psychodynamic therapies These focus on the unconscious relationship patterns that have evolved from childhood.
Humanistic therapies These focus on self-development in the 'here and now'.

QUICK FIX: GETTING HELP

There is no such thing as a quick fix when it comes to counselling or psychotherapy; it will take time to explore your feelings and talk about your problems. But there is a quick way to tap into the help you might need: visit *www.counselling-directory.org.uk* for more details and to find lists of qualified and registered professionals.

SUMMARY: PART FIVE TAKE ON THE HARDER TASKS

41 **Stay fit; keep it fun** Make your exercise sessions learning experiences too.

42 **Dive right in** Aim to immerse yourself in a task without thinking about it for too long; it is rarely as bad as you think it's going to be.

43 **Listen to yourself** Record your reasons for not getting started on a job; you may be surprised by how feeble they are.

44 **Team up on your way to achievement** For your long-term success, it may be mutually beneficial to form a partnership with someone.

45 **Delegate or die** Instructing others to assist you can enable you to capitalize on your strengths and shore up your weaknesses.

46 **Do one thing at a time** Multitaskers often end up avoiding the one key task that must be completed among the many.

47 **Apply the heavy half mentality** Once you get beyond the halfway point it's easier to finish the job.

48 **Employ the bigger and badder method** If you can identify a second task that is even more difficult than the first, you will have no problem getting started on the original job.

49 **Establish an escrow** Place a significant sum of money in another's safekeeping to be forfeited if you fail to meet your self-agreed deadlines.

50 **Seek counselling** When you have exhausted all other avenues of support, it may be time to seek professional help.

NOTES

part
six

part
six

SOAR TO GREAT HEIGHTS

SOLUTION 51
GET ORGANIZED ONE STEP AT A TIME

'A place for everything and everything in its place.'
Traditional saying

In a society increasingly overloaded with information, it is essential that you are organized in all aspects of your life, both at home and at work. You will hear people say that being organized takes too much time, but they should consider how much time disorganization has cost them. The information onslaught is only going to get worse; don't face the future with poor organizational skills.

break the overall task down into smaller tasks that are easy to complete in short bursts of activity

THE DIVIDE AND CONQUER PRINCIPLE

When it comes to tackling a paper backlog, avoid the 'all or nothing' approach that there is no point in getting started if you can't begin and finish the task in one go. This only serves to give you an excuse to put the job off yet again. When you approach the task with a 'divide and conquer' mindset, you are likely to be more productive. Break the overall task down into smaller tasks that are easy to complete in short bursts of activity. This way, slowly but surely, the job will get done.

GETTING A JOB DONE

Say, for example, you want to organize your desk drawers. Rather than tackling the whole job once, break it down into smaller tasks, handling one-half of one drawer at a time. Pick a reasonable goal of organizing the first half of one drawer this week, and tackle each half-drawer in subsequent weeks. In a few weeks the job will be done. If you are concerned about the length of time the job will take to complete, remember that 'weeks' is a lot sooner than 'never'.

QUICK FIX: 10-MINUTE TASKING

Break any job down into several tasks, none of which should take longer than 10 minutes to complete. Tackle one 10-minute task at a time. You'll find that when you tackle a 10-minute job, and gain the satisfaction of having completed it, you have more energy, focus and direction to take on another 10-minute job, or even a third. In this way, the overall job will be finished in no time at all.

SOLUTION 52
COVER THE CLOCK

'I go at what I am about as if there was nothing else in the world for the time being.'
Charles Kingsley

Time watching is one of the many distractions of the workplace. If possible, when trying to get started on a new project, try to avoid wearing a watch, or position yourself so that you are not constantly looking at the clock. This gives you the opportunity to focus your attention on the job at hand rather than counting yourself down to your next break.

When you take off your watch, you have a better chance of operating at your natural rhythm, which is a far more productive mode than when you monitor yourself by clock time.

staring at the clock won't make lunchtime come any faster

For more advice on getting rid of distractions and disruptions, see Solutions 18 and 19.

The typical employee comes to work and immediately starts the countdown to the end of the working day. When the clock says 10.15am, it's time for her coffee break, but if she hadn't looked at the clock, she might not get coffee as she might not feel like it then, and she could have finished the job she was working on. If we don't know what time it is, we respond to our bodies' needs, not the clock's demands.

HOW LONG WILL IT TAKE?

When you start a task in view of the clock, you may find it off-putting, wondering to yourself, 'How long will it take?' Yet, if you hide the clock until the job is completed, you may be surprised by how little time has passed. We've all experienced this phenomenon on one occasion or another. Time seems to slow down when we are highly focused and we are not conscious of it passing. If you hide the clock, big tasks won't seem quite as daunting as you believe them to be.

QUICK FIX: KEEPING TRACK OF TIME

If you have scheduled appointments that you need to get to, how do you remind yourself of the start time without a timepiece to hand? Here are a few ideas for how you can keep your focus but still be punctual:

- Ask a colleague who is also attending the meeting to give you a call 5 minutes before the start time.
- Set your watch alarm and pop it in your desk drawer.
- Set up an electronic reminder on your computer to prompt you when an appointment is due.

SOLUTION 53
ASSESS THE EFFECTS ON OTHERS

'Those who stand for nothing fall for anything.'
Alexander Hamilton

Your colleagues rely on you to do your job so they can do theirs. Picture who they are, and the effect your progress on a task or project will have on them. Imagine their anxiety and trepidation as they wait for you to come through with the goods. This focus on others' needs is a great motivator.

people are counting on you

It is easier to stay on track when you can relate your responsibilities to how they contribute to the progress of your team, division, department, organization or society in general (see Solution 4). Conversely, it is harder to get started when you are working alone, disconnected from others, unaware of the impact your work has. You need to acknowledge that your co-workers are counting on you to one degree or another.

QUICK FIX: GET WHAT YOU NEED

Just as others are relying on you to get a job done, you are relying on others to do theirs. If you need input from a colleague in order to meet a deadline, ensure that you:

Give them plenty of warning They'll have priorities of their own.
Provide a written brief Be as clear as you can.
Set a date Make this a few days earlier than your critical date.
Send a reminder A quick email a couple of days before the due date.

SOLUTION 54
MAKE SURE SOMEONE IS EXPECTING YOUR WORK

'In order that people may be happy in their work, these three things are needed. They must be fit for it, they must not do too much of it, and they must have a sense of success in it.'

John Ruskin

When given the chance to push back a job's timeline, most people take the opportunity to do so. Yet, when a completion time is ironclad, the do-it-or-else variety, you tend to get the task done, particularly when your boss is waiting for your completed work. In fact, your ability to start and complete a task is significantly increased if somebody is waiting on your progress.

The wise employee will recognize the value of a deadline rather than regarding it as a ball-and-chain that weighs him down. Routine deadlines, such as the weekly report, provide a structure against which he can measure his progress; and, if he wants to keep his job, thrive in his position and look forward to advancement, he needs to complete tasks to deadline. Without deadlines, he would accomplish much less. (For more on the power of deadlines, see Solution 55.)

QUICK FIX: FIND A BOSS

To help motivate you to complete a task, ask a friend to act as your boss. Get her to check the job after it has been completed and ask her to set you a deadline. You will find that having to report on your progress to someone will increase your odds of starting and finishing a job in a timely manner.

SOLUTION 55
GRASP THE POWER OF DEADLINES

'Seize the day, put no trust in tomorrow.'
Horace

Most people dread having to work to a deadline. Yet, if used correctly, the deadline can serve a very worthwhile purpose: it can enable you to marshal your resources towards accomplishing tasks that you might otherwise not get done.

There is a danger, however, that you might use a deadline to put off starting a job till a later date, telling yourself, 'I work better under pressure so I don't need to do this now.' Don't fool yourself into believing this, as it can result in unnecessary stress and a disappointed boss.

DEADLINES ARE OPPORTUNITIES FOR SUCCESS

Just as you can reframe a task or project and see it in a different light

The human body functions best when routines are established, such as sleeping for the same number of hours each night, eating at certain times throughout the day, and exercising at regular intervals throughout the week. Work, too, provides us with a structure to achieve our best, and working to deadline has a part to play. Consider the case of the employee who eagerly looks forward to his retirement. The big day arrives and is met with joy and celebration. Yet, just a few months – or even weeks – later he is missing the challenges of the workplace: with no one to report to, no projects to submit and no deadlines to meet, the days can drag on.

deadline a time limit for any activity

(see Solution 3), you can reframe the notion of deadlines so that you view them not for your potential for failure, but as your opportunity for success. Learn to use them to your advantage, to:

- Realize your achievements
- Establish or maintain positive routines
- Increase your productivity
- Be more profitable and competitive
- Be more energetic, vibrant and alert

QUICK FIX: SETTING DEADLINES

There are several software programs available to assist you in setting and keeping to effective deadlines. Try:

Task management software *www.mylifeorganized.net*
This software is designed to help you stay on top of your busy schedule. In a Windows or Pocket PC version, it will generate a to-do list with the steps necessary to complete your goals, and the list of next actions will be sorted in order of priority to keep you focused on the most important tasks.

VIP software *www.vip-qualitysoft.com/time_management/procrastination*
This will notify you by email, phone or pop-up when a deadline is approaching. The program also has the capability to help you estimate the time required and the difficulty of different tasks more realistically.

SOLUTION 56
STOP MULTITASKING

'For him who has no concentration, there is no tranquillity.'
The Bhagavad Gita

Despite the advantages of working on one thing at a time (see Solution 46), we all tend to multitask, tricking ourselves into thinking that by doing several things at once, we're getting more done. We couldn't be further from the truth.

THE DANGERS OF MULTITASKING

don't fall into the trap of routinely doubling up on activities in the quest to get more done

You probably multitask more than you care to admit. Most multitasking activities seem pretty harmless, such as surfing the internet while watching TV, reading while eating, talking on the phone while doodling, or listening to music while studying.

Others are positively dangerous, such as putting on your make-up while driving to work, or using a chainsaw while taking a call on your mobile phone. Yet all multitasking has an impact on your productivity. When you switch tasks, you interrupt your thought processes and lose valuable time. To ensure that you complete more of what you want or need to accomplish, you need to safeguard, nurture and support your focus on the task at hand.

multitasking
switching back
and forth between
activities of varying
complexity

THE BENEFITS OF DOING ONE THING AT A TIME

When you initiate a project, you need to give your full and undivided attention to the task at hand to have the best chance of doing a good and timely job. If you fall into the trap of believing that you can handle several things at once, the chances are that you will restrict yourself to working only on those tasks that are comfortable, familiar and easy for you. These are probably not the tasks that will help you to advance in your career.

If you multitask:
- You are more likely to put things off.
- You'll constantly be bumping up against work deadlines.
- You will be making up excuses for putting off the challenging yet more rewarding projects.
- You will overtax everyone around you, including yourself.

If you stop multitasking:
- You'll be less likely to put off getting started on a project.
- Your ability to get things done on time will improve.
- People will want to work with you.
- You can leave at the end of the day with a sense of accomplishment.

give your full and undivided attention to the task at hand

QUICK FIX: MULTITASKING

For those of you who are still convinced that you can achieve more by trying to do several things at once, take on board this advice: it's easier to juggle four tennis balls than three tennis balls and a banana.

SOLUTION 57
POST YOUR PROBLEM

'Nothing in this world can take the place of persistence.'
Calvin Coolidge

Here's a procrastination-blasting technique that requires only a few minutes to set up and works well for many people. When you have something you need to do, remind yourself to do it by putting Post-it notes all around the office and even around the home.

post numerous reminders so that as you go about your day you can't help but encounter them

A friend of mine needed to clean the coils on the back of her refrigerator. So, she posted a note on the refrigerator door. After several days of seeing the note, she decided to temporarily put it on top of the refrigerator. As you might guess, weeks passed without her handling the task. One day, while dusting, she encountered the note. Realizing that she had put off the task of cleaning the coils for weeks, she reposted the note on the front door of the refrigerator. Sure enough, two days later, she tackled and completed the job.

HOW DOES IT WORK?

Posting your challenges, big and small, is an effective technique for overcoming procrastination. Repeatedly encountering these messages will eventually have an effect, and these not-so-subtle reminders will spur you into action. For this strategy to work, you must not hide or remove the messages until you have completed the task. In this case, 'out of sight' really does mean 'out of mind'.

QUICK FIX: TIDY YOUR DESK

As you never know which encounter with one of your reminder messages will serve as the final catalyst to prompt you to get started, it is important to post as many as you can. Write the reminder 'CLEAN OUT DESK' on several Post-it notes and place:

- One on the desk drawer
- One on the filing cabinet
- One on your telephone
- One on your appointment book
- One on the side of your bookcase
- One on the inside of your office door
- One on the dashboard of your car
- One on your bedside table
- One on your alarm clock

SOLUTION 58
DECREASE DOWNTIME

'Success seems to be largely a matter of hanging on after others have let go.'
William Feather

While it is important to take some time for relaxation and recreation (see Solutions 32 and 33), it is just as important to guard against taking breaks just for the sake of it (Solution 52). If you are not careful, downtime becomes just another excuse for not getting on with the task in hand.

a short break to check email often leads to an hour of catching up

SCHEDULED BREAKS

When working intensively on a task, for example when studying for an exam, it can be sensible to schedule break times. A 50-minute period of concentration, say, could be followed by a 10-minute period of rest. But do not let too much downtime affect your productivity. Be aware that problems can occur when:

- Breaks extend past the allotted time interval
- Rest periods are scheduled too frequently
- Downtime is used as an excuse for not getting started on your next task
- Interruptions disturb your concentration and prevent you from getting back into the project
- Diversions invite you to deviate from your intended goals
- Pausing becomes your semi-permanent state

DON'T TAKE A BREAK JUST FOR THE SAKE OF IT

Rather than scheduling breaks, it might prove more productive if you take a break only when you feel the need to do so (see Solution 52). When you have finally mustered the resolve to handle a task that you have been putting off, let your energy level be your guide as to when to rest. If, for example, you are on a roll it makes sense to forgo a planned break, so that you don't break your working rhythm. You'll know instinctively when the time is right to pause and, if you are honest with yourself, when to get back to work too.

on a roll
experiencing a period of success or good luck, based on the idea that something that is rolling tends to continue rolling

QUICK FIX: GETTING THROUGH MORE

Short breaks can help you motivate yourself to tackle a series of small tasks that you have been putting off. Suppose you have five 3- to 5-minute tasks to do. Give yourself a 2-minute break between each task. Alternatively, complete three tasks, take a 4-minute break, then complete the final two tasks. Yet again, you may find that the 'buzz' of completing each task prompts you to start the next one without taking a break at all. See what works best for you.

SOLUTION 59
MANAGE YOUR LIFE ONE DAY AT A TIME

'The best thing about the future is that it comes only one day at a time.'
Abraham Lincoln

To plan for and to achieve the big goals you need to accomplish, you must start thinking in day units. A 'day unit' is a convenient measure for charting progress and can help to keep you motivated. When you work in day units, particularly on a large project, even the most challenging of tasks seems achievable.

accomplish today's work today and tend to tomorrow's affairs tomorrow

A foreman in a manufacturing plant dreams of becoming a movie scriptwriter. He has set himself a three-year goal to make the transition. He has established a daily goal of spending a minimum of 15 minutes a day working on his scripts. Some evenings he is able to get two or three pages completed; other days, he is only able to produce a paragraph. He also attends scriptwriting seminars and workshops, reads articles and books on the topic, and even attends meetings of a scriptwriters' association. Eighteen months in, he is still working full-time as a foreman, yet he is enthusiastic about the progress he is making and he is maintaining focus, one day at a time, for his ultimate goal of becoming a full-time scriptwriter.

THE DAY UNIT COUNTING METHOD

day

units a way to measure the time required to achieve a goal – you can count 6 hours of steady work as a day

For everyday situations, plan for 6 hours of concentrated, focused work a day, leaving you with about 2 hours for administration, correspondence and rest breaks. Now estimate how many day units you'll need to complete a large project, factoring in weekends, holidays and other downtime. The figure you derive will be a manageable, meaningful guide for monitoring your progress.

It is worth noting that many project management software programs enable you to monitor your progress or make adjustments when unforeseen developments arise. If you fall behind on your project you can readjust accordingly, and on those occasions when you get ahead with a project, you can allocate resources more judiciously than you did initially.

QUICK FIX: MAINTAINING FOCUS ON LONG-TERM PROJECTS

Procrastination is more likely to occur on projects that last several weeks or months. If considerable effort brings you only slightly closer to the project's completion, it may be difficult to see how activities on any given day contribute to your long-term progress. To help keep you moving forwards, it will help to devote a fixed time each day to work for a minimum period on your long-term project, for example 30 minutes at midday.

SOLUTION 60
IGNORE YOUR AGE

'How old would you be if you didn't know how old you were?'
Satchel Paige

Whether you are 20 or 60 years old, or somewhere in between, anytime is a good time to get started on what you seek to accomplish. It's never too late to begin. All entrepreneurs share the same skills and characteristics, whatever age they may be: a compelling vision, a flair for business, perseverance, positive self-regard, energy and a passion to succeed. At 60, the energy level may not be what it was at 20, but the rest still holds true. Energy is overrated – it's the life experience that gets you ahead.

don't be afraid to start something new whatever stage of life you are at – it's never too late to succeed

James Michener didn't write his first novel until he was 42, the same age Elvis died; Michener then produced one bestseller after another until his death at the age of 90. The late Jessica Tandy won the Academy Award for Best Actress at 80. Colonel Sanders of Kentucky Fried Chicken fame didn't launch his business until the age of 65, using his first social security payment as his start-up funds. All this just goes to show that you are never too old to succeed.

QUICK FIX: LIFE ASPIRATIONS

Alyce Cornyn-Selby, a prolific author and speaker from Portland, Oregon, uses this exercise to blast through the procrastination that sometimes accompanies big projects and lifelong aspirations. Write the sentence:

'I have now come to the end of my life and I'm disappointed that I didn't........................'

Do this exercise ten times. Don't think too hard about it. Just write down what readily comes to mind. How did you finish that sentence? Whatever you came up with first is probably something you want to do right away.

Alternatively, imagine the alternative scenario and write the sentence:

'I have now come to the end of my life and I'm glad that I ....'

What did you come up with this time? Was it the same issue that you addressed in the first statement? Was it something you have already accomplished? When you begin to look at the opportunities that await you and those that you can create for yourself, procrastination will become a thing of the past.

be comfortable with your age and recognize the vast potential you have with all your remaining years

SUMMARY: PART SIX
SOAR TO GREAT HEIGHTS

51 **Get organized one step at a time** Break a task down into a series of smaller tasks that are easy to complete in short bursts of activity.

52 **Cover the clock** Focus your attention on the job at hand rather than counting yourself down to your next break.

53 **Assess the effects on others** Acknowledge that your colleagues are relying on you to get your job done so that they can do theirs.

54 **Make sure someone is expecting your work** Your ability to start and complete a task is significantly increased if somebody is waiting on your progress.

55 **Grasp the power of deadlines** Setting a time limit for an activity will enable you to marshal your resources towards accomplishing tasks that you might otherwise not get done.

56   **Stop multitasking** You need to give your full and undivided attention to the task at hand to have the best chance of doing a good and timely job.

57   **Post your problem** Remind yourself that you have a job to do by putting Post-it notes all around the office and even around the home; these not-so-subtle reminders will spur you into action.

58   **Decrease downtime** Be on your guard that the rest periods you take do not become just another excuse for not getting on with the task in hand.

59   **Manage your life one day at a time** To stay motivated on long-term projects that may take many weeks to complete, devote a fixed time slot every day to focus on these tasks.

60   **Ignore your age** Don't be afraid to start something new whatever stage of life you are at – it's never too late to succeed.

NOTES

FURTHER READING

Assagioli, Roberto, *The Act of Will* (Viking Press, 1973)

Ayan, Jordan, *Aha! 10 Ways to Free Your Creative Spirit and Find Your Great Ideas* (Crown, 1997)

Blakeslee, Thomas, *Beyond the Conscious Mind* (Plenum Press, 1996)

Bliss, Edwin C., *Doing It Now: A Twelve-Step Program for Curing Procrastination and Achieving Your Goals* (Scribner, 1983)

Breininger, Dorothy and Debby S. Bitticks, *Time Efficiency Makeover: Own Your Time and Your Life by Conquering Procrastination* (HCI, 2005)

Burka, Jane and Lenora M. Wuen, *Procrastination: Why You Do It, What to Do About It.* 3rd Ed. (Addison-Wesley, 2004)

Cameron, Julia, *The Artist's Way* (Jeremy P. Tarcher/Perigee, 1992)

Caroselli, Marlene, *Defeating Procrastination: 52 Fail-Safe Tips for Keeping Time on Your Side* (SkillPath, 1997)

Cathcart, Jim, *The Acorn Principle* (St Martin's, 1998)

Conwell, Russell H., *Acres of Diamonds* (Jove, 1995)

Csikszentmihalyi, Mihaly, *Flow: The Psychology of Optimal Experience* (Harper & Row, 1990)

Daniels, Aubrey, *Bringing Out the Best in People* (McGraw-Hill, 2000)

Davidson, Jeff, *Breathing Space: Living & Working at a Comfortable Pace in a Sped-up Society* (Booksurge, 2007)

Davidson, Jeff, *The Complete Idiot's Guide to Reaching Your Goals* (Alpha Books, 1998)

Dawson, Roger, *The 13 Secrets of Power Performance* (Prentice-Hall, 1994)

Douglas, Mack R., *How to Make a Habit of Succeeding* (Zondervan, 1972)

Drucker, Peter F., *The Effective Executive* (Harper & Row, 1967)

Dyer, Wayne W., *How to Be a No Limit Person* (Berkley, 1980)

Emmett, Rita, *The Procrastinator's Handbook* (Walker, 2000)

Everett, Henry C., *How to Reach Your Goals: How to Conquer Procrastination, Fear, and Other Obstacles on Your Way* (Universe.com, 2000)

Fiore, Neil, *The Now Habit: A Strategic Program for Overcoming Procrastination and Enjoying Guilt-Free Play* (Tarcher, 2007)

Freeman, Dave, Neil Teplica, and the editors of WhatsGoingOn.com with Jennifer Coonce, *100 Things to Do Before You Die: Travel Events You Just Can't Miss* (Taylor Publishing, 1999)

Friedan, Betty, *The Fountain of Age* (Simon & Schuster, 1993)

Fritz, Robert, *The Path of Least Resistance* (Fawcett, 1989)

Fulghum, Robert, *All I Really Need to Know I Learned in Kindergarten* (Fawcett, 1993)

Goleman, Daniel, *Emotional Intelligence* (Bantam, 1995)

Helmstetter, Shad, *What to Say When You Talk to Yourself* (Pocket Books, 1990)

Horney, Karen, *Neurosis and Human Growth* (Norton, 1991)

Jeffers, Susan, *Feel the Fear and Do It Anyway* (Fawcett Books, 1992)

Jolley, Willie, *A Setback Is a Setup for a Comeback* (St Martin's, 1999)

Knaus, William J., *Do It Now! Break the Procrastination Habit* (J. Wiley, 1998)

Knaus, William J., *Do It Now: How To Stop Procrastinating* (Prentice-Hall, 1979)

Koenig, Larry J., *Getting Things Done Now: 17 Proven Principles For Overcoming Procrastination* (Thomas Nelson Publishers, 2006)

Lakein, Alan, *How to Get Control of Your Time and Your Life* (P.H. Wyden, 1973)

Lively, Lynn, *The Procrastinator's Guide to Success* (McGraw-Hill, 1999)

Maltz, Maxwell, *Psycho-cybernetics* (Pocket Books, 1989)

Pagonis, William G., with Jeffrey L. Cruikshank. *Moving Mountains* (Harvard Business School Press, 1992)

Porat, Frieda, *Creative Procrastination: Organizing Your Own Life* (Harper & Row, 1980)

Roberts, Susan M., *Living Without Procrastination: How to Stop Postponing Your Life* (New Harbinger, 1995)

Salsbury, Glenna, *The Art of the Fresh Start* (Health Communications, 1995)

Sapadin, Linda and Jack Maguire, *It's About Time! The Six Styles of Procrastination and How to Overcome Them* (Penguin, 1997)

Sugarman, Joseph, *Success Forces* (Contemporary Books, 1980)

Tracy, Brian, *Eat That Frog! 21 Great Ways to Stop Procrastinating and Get More Done in Less Time* (Berrett-Koehler, 2007)

Tullier, Michelle L., *The Complete Idiot's Guide to Overcoming Procrastination* (Alpha Books, 1999)

Viscott, David S., *Emotional Resilience* (Crown, 1997)

Watson, Donna, *101 Simple Ways to Be Good to Yourself: How to Discover Peace and Joy in Your Life* (Bard, 1992)

ABOUT THE AUTHOR

JEFF DAVIDSON is an author and professional speaker who offers new perspectives and fresh solutions to the career and life balance problems that people face today. He has been featured in the USA's top newspapers including *USA Today*, the *Washington Post*, the *New York Times*, the *Los Angeles Times* and the *Chicago Tribune*. A five-time state winner of the US Small Business Administration's Media Advocate of the Year Award, he has published more than 3,550 articles on the topics of life-balance, management and marketing effectiveness, and time management. Corporate clients who have benefited from his expertise include America Online, Lufthansa, Wells Fargo, NationsBank, IBM, Swissotel, Executone, American Express, and more than 500 other leading organizations and associations including the US Treasury.

Jeff is a columnist in three publications, an audio columnist on Selling Power Live, and a frequent Webinar presenter for the Manage Smarter, Audio Educators and Apex Performance Systems. In the highly competitive field of self-help, business and how-to books, sales of his books exceed over 100,000 copies sold in the last five years alone, and his output includes such popular titles as: *The Joy of Simple Living*, *The Complete Guide to Public Speaking*, *Breathing Space* and *The Complete Idiot's Guide to Time Management*.

For more information on Jeff and his work, visit *www.BreathingSpace.com* or contact him by email at *Jeff@BreathingSpace.com*.

INDEX